Energy in Transition

Energy in Transition

A Report on Energy Policy and Future Options

Måns Lönnroth, Peter Steen, and Thomas Johansson

University of California Press
Berkeley, Los Angeles, London

University of California Press
Berkeley and Los Angeles, California
University of California Press, Ltd.
London, England
Copyright © 1980 by The Regents of the University of California
ISBN 0-520-03881-9
Library of Congress Catalog Card Number: 78-68827
Printed in the United States of America

1   2   3   4   5   6   7   8   9

Contents

Preface   vii

Energy and Society: An American View
   by Lee Schipper   xi

Introduction: the connecting thread   1

1 Swedish energy policy: today, yesterday, tomorrow   3

2 Getting away from today's energy systems   9
   Introduction   9
   The flow of energy on earth   9
   Society, energy use, and welfare   12
   Society's energy sources   14

3 Toward tomorrow's energy systems   21
   Historical transitions of energy sources   21
   Conceivable future energy sources   24
   The transition: time perspective, mechanisms, and
     distribution of powers   29
   The terms of transition   35

4 Limits to freedom of action   43
   Introduction   43
   How much energy do we really need?   46
   What types of energy do we need?   48
   Can we control the energy supply system?   50

5 Energy policy: on goal conflicts in social organization   54
   Introduction   54
   Energy and economics   56
   Energy and environment   73
   Energy and geographic structure   77
   Energy and foreign policy   81

6 Choice of energy carriers and freedom of action in energy policy   87

Introduction   87

Energy quality   88

The choice of energy carriers   91

Alternative energy systems   94

7 Energy and social organization   98

Introduction   98

The dynamics of technological change: some attitudes about how technologies are chosen   99

Technical and organizational change: example from the electricity sector   102

Expansion: is it built in?   109

Organizations and uncertainty   113

A few words about the interorganizational system of rules   116

On the role of Parliament and Cabinet   121

Supporting activities required for the various solutions   124

Organizational design for freedom of action: is there one?   126

8 Nuclear power in Sweden's energy future: commitments and alternatives   136

Introduction   136

Establishing nuclear power: pushing and pulling   136

Swedish energy policy in the '70s: from consent to dissent   139

Long-term supply alternatives   144

Solar Sweden   149

Interrupting the momentum   158

Politics of an open-ended policy   162

Bibliography   165

Index   169

Preface

UPON RECOMMENDATION of a royal commission chaired by Alva Myrdal, then minister of disarmament in the Swedish government, the Secretariat for Future Studies was organized in 1973. The commission report was published in 1972 and has been translated into English ("To choose a future").

The Secretariat for Future Studies was attached originally to the prime minister's office. In 1975 an executive committee was appointed, consisting of members representing all political parties in the Swedish Parliament. This committee and the Secretariat are now attached administratively to the Ministry of Education.

So far the Secretariat has sponsored six large projects and two limited ones. The first four of these, which were started in 1974-75, "Energy and Society," "Sweden in World Society," "Resources and Raw Materials," and "Working Life in the Future" were completed during 1977-78.

Projects are organized as research teams with strong links to various ministries, but formally each is independent. Roughly four or five professionals are employed on a full-time basis along with part-time consultants recruited mainly from the universities. The links to the ministries are in the form of reference groups, where analyses, background material, and so forth are discussed. Final conclusions, however, are the responsibility of the project groups alone. Money is granted at the start; projects usually run two or three years.

The project, "Energy and Society," was originated in 1974, with work starting in 1975. A series of reports has been published, covering various topics, such as energy and economic growth, various environmental factors, energy analysis, the nuclear fuel cycle, and alternative energy sources such as oil, coal, and the like, the history of Swedish energy policy, and the possibilities of placing Sweden entirely on a solar energy basis, among others. All are published in Swedish, but some material is also available inEnglish. The final report "Solar versus nuclear—choosing energy futures" was published in Swedish during the summer of 1978 and in English (by Pergamon Press) in 1980.

The reports are circulated through a subscription system to a fairly large readership, ranging from government agencies, members of Parliament, political parties, and schools to newspapers, private companies, and individuals. Moreover, press coverage has been rather substantial.

This book consists of three parts. The first is a short essay, written by Lee Schipper, on the possible use of the Swedish experience for the United States. The second, and main, part is the midterm report of the project published in Swedish at the end of 1976. It lays out a conceptual framework for looking at long-term energy policy. The third and final part is a recent essay on the role of nuclear power in Sweden, both in the present political process and in the longer time perspective of energy policy. It is based both on official Swedish studies and on work done in the project subsequent to the publishing of the midterm report. The third part also contains a short summary of some of the main conclusions of the final report, such as the possibilities of placing Sweden exclusively on solar energy.

It should be emphasized, however, that the basic aim of the project has not been to make long-term forecasts or predictions, but rather to develop a framework for looking at energy policy as a long-term problem. The view is that long-term problems are as much conceptual as they are technical and economic, and that much more effort should be directed toward understanding the basic nature of these problems. One major reason for this approach is that in the latest decision on Swedish energy policy, made in May 1975, the concept of freedom of action and the problem of how to avoid foreclosing future options were stressed. As we see it, the subsequent course of debate on energy policy in Sweden has confirmed the basic soundness of this approach. Since 1975, two governments have foundered over the issue of energy policy in general and nuclear energy policy in particular. There is no sign that political pressure is diminishing; energy probably will continue to play an important part in Swedish politics. In March 1980 a referendum will be held on nuclear energy.

Considering the great technical, economic, and environmental uncertainties about future supply alternatives—be they fossil, nuclear, or renewable—policy must be oriented toward avoiding bad solutions rather than trying to choose optimal ones today. Therefore, the main thrust is to understand the mechanisms that commit societies to one or another supply alternative, to learn to change such mechanisms, and to keep several doors open at once.

Obviously, these topics cannot be discussed fully in a single booklet. The same is true for topics covered in other project reports. However, we operate on the general philosophy that at this stage it is more important to introduce one or two new ideas into the debate than to come up with the final feasible answer. At times, therefore, this report is rather provocative, the better to stimulate further debate and suggest more detailed studies.

We think that the reasoning and findings in this report are sufficiently general to be of interest not only to a small, prosperous country like Sweden, which depends heavily on imported oil, but to other nations also.

Måns Lönnroth, Thomas B. Johansson, and Peter Steen are chiefly responsible for parts II and III of this book. Much of its contents are based on the contributions of others who have written more specialized articles. In particular, the authors want to thank Lars Bergman, Bo Diczfalusy (chapter 5), Hans Esping (chapter

7 in Part II and sections 5 and 6 in Part III). Finally, our appreciation to Margareta Grånäs for the many drafts she typed.

Stockholm, January 1979
Secretariat for Future Studies

Måns Lönnroth
Project leader

Lars Ingelstam
Executive secretary

1 Swedish krona (Skr)	= US $0.24 or £0.14 (approx.)
1 kilogram (kg)	= 2.2 pounds
1 ton	= 1,000 kilograms
1 ton of oil	= 7.4 US barrels of oil (average value)
1 cubic meter (m³)	= 35.3 cubic feet (= 6.3 US barrels)
1 kilometer (km)	= 1,000 meters
1 hectare (ha)	= 2.5 acres
1 megawatt hour (MWh)	= 1,000 kilowatt hours (kWh)(= 3.413 x 10^6 BTU)
1 terawatt hour (TWh)	= 1 million MWh
1 toe	= energy amount equivalent to 1 ton of oil
1 Mtoe (1 million toe)	= energy amount equivalent to 1 ton of oil
1 Mtoe (1 million toe)	= 11.6 TWh
1 Q (Quad)	= 10^{15} BTU = 293 TWh

Energy and Society: An American View

by
Lee Schipper

HAVEN'T WE HEARD enough about Sweden? In the case of energy, probably not. This is because the structure of demand for energy in Sweden is more like that in America than in any other country. And the depth of the debate over society's choices for long-term energy sources is equally great in the United States and Sweden, while less intense anywhere else.

Background: Swedish and American Energy Uses Compared

Much of what has concerned Lönnroth and his colleagues in the research project on energy and society deals with various aspects of energy supply. For example, the energy debate in both Sweden and the United States often focuses upon issues of nuclear safety or the role of large energy-production corporations in the energy future of both nations. Måns Lönnroth and his coauthors, however, have shown us clearly that it is hard to discuss energy supplies alone. So much of society's structure today is bound up with the way energy is *used* that this less-understood side of the energy debate in fact may be *more* important. As the reader will see, *Energy in Transition* points to the many ways in which energy supply and demand are institutionally and technologically linked far beyond their interaction in the marketplace. Society, therefore, should concern itself equally with these two sides of the energy debate.

Before reading any further about energy and (Swedish) society, however, it might be helpful to review certain aspects of energy use in Sweden, with a particular view toward comparing them to similar uses in the United States.

The most important differences between energy use in Sweden and the United States can be summarized as differences in what goes in—much more oil, relatively speaking, in Sweden than in America—and *how much* goes in—a lot less, reckoned in terms of per capita use, or consumption of all energy per unit of economic activity. Oil so predominates as the primary fuel in Scandinavia that in the early 1970s Sweden was the world's largest per capita consumer of that fuel.

At the same time, Sweden has been endowed historically with free-flowing water that could be converted cheaply into electricity. But in the late 1960s it was discovered that even hydropower was not really cheap, because of the costs to the environment wrought by the presence of dams.

It was at that time thought, however, that nuclear power would begin to provide electricity so cheap that metering would not be necessary. Many reckoned that with inexpensive electricity and apparently unlimited oil, energy consumption could grow regardless of cost and, in fact, consumption in Sweden in the 1960s grew far faster than in America. Automobiles, single family dwellings, and consumer goods began to appear in ever increasing abundance.

The 1973 oil embargo reminded us that oil was not in unending supply, and no longer cheap. Meanwhile, the debate over nuclear power, which has been particularly intense in Sweden, focused attention on the fact that the atom was costing us far more than we had been promised. With nuclear power questionable, hydroelectricity drying up in many ways, coal almost too dirty to burn, and all those other sources not quite ready to take over, the concern over energy in Sweden was understandable.

America, by contrast, has been rich in all the basic energy fuels. Here the debate centers more on how much to pay for each source and how much will be left over next year. In 1977 the United States imported half its oil; this in turn amounted to around 25 percent of all energy consumed, compared with a figure of 60-75 percent for Scandanavia as a whole. This means that sudden rises in the price of world energy supplies could have a more marked effect on the economies and lifestyles of Scandinavians than of Americans. Indeed, the effect of indecision over energy in the United States has been to smooth out the consequences of the quadrupling of the world price of oil even as the imported share of American energy consumption itself grew from 10 percent to its present quarter. Americans, who paid considerably less for energy than Scandinavians before the oil embargo, still pay considerably less six years later, because of natural endowments and policies that have kept prices down. These differences in energy prices suggest that patterns of energy use also will differ considerably.

Contrasts in Energy Use

After looking into these differences with my colleague, Allan Lichtenberg, many of the data on energy use began to appear. We found the following to be characteristic of the differences (See table 1):

A. Energy use per unit of Gross National Product, while a poor measure of anything, nevertheless reflected less efficient use in the United States, where it is highest, followed by Norway, Sweden, then Denmark and Finland.

B. This crude measure of effectiveness must be adjusted for many factors. Sweden, for example, *exports* products requiring far more energy for manufacture than her imports do. Denmark is the exact opposite, and the United States is about in balance.

C. Climate in Scandinavia is an extremely important factor in energy use. Heating of factories, alone, while insignificant in the United States, is as great in Sweden (per capita) as is air conditioning here!

TABLE 1
SWEDISH AND AMERICAN ENERGY CONSUMPTION 1971

Consumption	United States			Sweden		
	kWh	kWhe	kWht	kWh	kWhe	kWht
Transportation	24,025	25	24,075	7,350	200	7,775
Commercial	9,600	2,150	14,250	7,375	1,500	10,625
Residential	13,500	2,300	18,450	11,125	1,400	14,150
Industry	28,900	3,300	36,000	20,400	4,200	29,450
Feedstocks	5,600		5,600	2,500		2,500
Utility losses	14,200			3,700		
Actual Consumption	95,825	7,775	98,375	52,450	7,300	64,500
Energy embodied in foreign trade	1,800		1,800	-4,600		-4,600
Net consumption	97,625	7,775	100,175	48,150	7,300	59,900

The table breaks down Swedish and American energy consumption per capita amounts allocated to the most common sectors. The column labeled kWhe shows electricity use per capita, while the column kWh shows total energy use including electricity. In the third column electricity is counted according to the amount of fuel required for its production; this tends to distort Swedish data since most electricity in 1971 was produced by hydropower. Using this table, however, the reader can count energy any way he feels. "Feedstocks" refer to the use of petroleum for nonfuel purposes; "energy embodied in foreign trade" gives an estimate of the energy required to produce the goods imported and exported by each country. The United States tends to import a small amount of this energy, while Sweden is a greater exporter.

D. Even the method of counting energy units affects comparisons. Hydropower is counted one way, electric power cogenerated with heat another way, and purely thermal electric power, by far the dominant source in the United States, is counted yet another way.

E. Finally, the makeup of economic output in each country differs. In Norway and Sweden the mix of products produced requires more energy *intrinsically* than those produced in the United States. By contrast, the extractive energy industry is far more important in the United States as a consumer of energy than it is anywhere in Scandinavia.

When all these adjustments and differences are compared, one striking fact remains. Energy use per unit of activity (e.g., per mile driven, per day heating, or per ton of raw material) is usually considerably lower in Scandinavia than in the United States. Using material drawn from our Swedish-American comparison, the following picture emerges (table 2 summarizes the differences found in the original study).

TRANSPORTATION

The most obvious distinctions occur here. In the United States autos are considerably (50 percent) more abundant per person *and* are about 80 percent less fuel-efficient measured in miles per gallon. Moreover, they tend to be driven more in the cities and in short hops than in Scandinavia. This pushes energy use up even further and steals riders from mass transit. Gasoline consumption per capita in the early '70s was thus almost three times greater in the United States than in Sweden; but automobile ownership there has been growing faster than in the United States, so the gap is closing somewhat. Moreover, miles driven per gallon have jumped dramatically in the United States and have started to rise again in Sweden as well.

Mass transit is considerably more important in Sweden in terms of passengers carried or share of all miles traveled, especially in the cities. On the whole, however, the automobile dominates land travel in *all* countries, accounting for 80 percent of all traffic in Sweden and over 90 percent in the United States. Airplane traffic, while not so important domestically in Sweden, because of geography and the survival of the rail system, is growing rapidly in international traffic as people there fly south for the winter.

On the freight side, trucks dominate energy demands for domestic hauling in Scandinavia and in the United States. Aside from cars, the only striking difference in efficiency we found in transportation was that light trucks in Sweden consumed far

TABLE 2
Contrasts between Swedish and American Energy Use
(Ratios)

	Per capita demand or production	Intensity	Total energy use	Notes
Autos	0.6	0.6	0.36	Swedish 24 MPG driving cycle uses less energy
Mass transit: trains, bus	2.9	0.80	2.35	Mass transit takes 40% of passenger miles in trips under 20 km in Sweden
Urban truck	0.95	0.3	0.28	Swedish trucks; smaller, more diesels
Residential space heat (energy/deg day x area)	(1.7x0.95)	0.5	0.81	Sweden 9200 deg days vs 5500 U.S. deg days
Appliances	?	?	0.55	U.S. more large appliances
Commercial total/sq meters	1.3	0.6	0.78	Air conditioning important in U.S. only
Heavy industry (physical basis)				Sweden more
Paper	4.2			electric intensive
Steel	1.1			because of cheap
Oil	0.5	0.6–0.9	0.92	hydroelectric
Cement	1.35			power. Also
Aluminum	0.5			Swedish
Chemicals	0.6			cogeneration
Light industry ($ V.A.)	0.67	0.6	0.4	Space heating significant in Sweden
Thermal generation of electricity	0.3	0.75	0.23	Swedish large hydroelectric cogeneration

fewer gallons/per ton mile of freight than in the United States. In absolute terms, the differences in consumption in the Scandinavian and American transportation sectors were the largest differences of all.

Housing and Buildings

Because of the severe winters, we expected to find energy use for heating far greater in Sweden than in the United States, but in fact the amounts were similar. This was due mainly to significantly better levels of insulation and more careful construction practices in Sweden. While far more Swedes than Americans live in apartments, little energy is saved by this difference because few apartments in Sweden are charged directly for actual use of heat, a serious economic as well as social problem: few apartment dwellers or owners have the incentive to conserve, meaning that levels of heating in practice were as high as in single family dwellings where the bills are paid by the user. Were it not for the significant levels of insulation in buildings in Sweden, the consumption of heat would be uneconomically high. This applies both to dwellings and to offices. Indeed, most observers find that indoor temperatures in Sweden are considerably higher than in the United States, at least in winter. This finding, usually ignored,

Table 2 provides a structural and efficiency breakdown of differences in energy use. The first column gives the ratio of per capita demand for the amenity or product listed (Sweden/United States). Since Americans drive farther per capita than Swedes, the first number, less than one, reflects an important difference in *structure*. The second column compares the relative amounts of energy/unit output (again Sweden/United States). Since it took roughly 60 percent as much energy per passenger mile to drive in Sweden, compared to the United States, and Swedes drove about 60 percent as much as Americans, the ratio of energy consumption is .6 x .6 or .36. Residential heating demand is broken down into two ratios, one reflecting the greater demand of the Swedish climate, the other reflecting the slightly smaller space/person in Swedish homes. Using a table such as this one, we can determine the extent to which conservation factors (intensity) as opposed to lifestyle or economic structure factors (per capita demand for an amenity) influence the total demand for energy in any country.

is important: it indicates that *behavioral* change—indoor heating habits—offers significant potential for energy conservation in otherwise "efficient" Sweden.

Appliances, on the other hand, are not as abundant as heat. While Swedes are not Spartan—all the basics are there—the abundance of appliances of the largest sizes common to American households has not yet arrived. Still, household use of electricity has been growing somewhat faster in Sweden than in the United States, reflecting recent rapid growth in incomes, which in turn stimulates the acquisition and use of gadgets. As incomes rose, the rapid increase in ownership and use of appliances, the acquisition of single family dwellings, and, indeed, the purchase of the first second automobile have occurred over a shorter period of time in Sweden than they did in the United States, meaning that many of the uses for energy that took years to appear in America sprang up almost over night in Sweden. Finally, in Sweden where taxes are high and interest is tax-deductible, many major purchases are made on credit. Even in 1979 automobiles and appliances were still selling well.

INDUSTRY

Because Sweden produces more tons of energy-thirsty materials, like paper and pulp, than the United States, energy-use totals in industry alone can be misleading. Sweden makes more cement on less fuel and electricity per ton than the United States, for example, although the total amounts of energy used are about the same per capita in each country. When similar comparisons of individual products or materials are made, the energy cost of making almost anything is less in Sweden than in the United States. In the wake of higher energy prices, all countries see the advantage in letting those nations with energy make the raw materials while concentrating themselves on refining those materials instead into high quality, higher-valued finished products. The truth is that high technology does not mean high

energy consumption, a fact already reflected in much of the structure of energy use in the United States.

Of course, there are many differences in energy use that are not
immediately reflected in these summaries. The lower use of gasoline in Sweden reflects less travel and fewer cars, an important
life-style distinction. Obviously the need for an automobile depends
on cultural, economic, and social factors that differ in the two
countries. Then again, the constant rush to make the bus, seen
everywhere in Stockholm, is far more hectic than the leisure that
having a car in downtown Los Angeles or San Francisco offers,
where parking is easier and streets more passable. Clearly the
energy and conservation implications of lifestyles are two-sided,
and while Americans move toward smaller cars used less frequently, the Swedes doubtlessly will move a little toward the
familiar American pattern—if for no other reason than to learn
the hard way.

Sometimes reasons, while surprising, are comprehensible. As
Lönnroth and his colleagues note, an automobile often becomes
a necessity these days in Sweden when both parents work and
their children are left in a child-care center far from home. Swedish taxes, which allow deductions for commuting expenses, recog-
nize the use of the car if it can be shown that forty-five minutes
is saved each way compared with taking the bus. Moreover,
Sweden offers many incentives for the purchase of single family
dwellings which, in the context of much higher marginal income
taxes, make that option more attractive every day. This creates
a population spread and thins out ridership in mass transit,
pushing up auto use even more. Finally, nearly half of the new
cars sold in Sweden are now registered with firms that allow their
employees this almost income tax-free way of driving. Thus, lifestyles in Sweden still are evolving in ways that will have a marked
effect on energy use in the 1980s and 1990s, even before conservation sets in.

In our study of Sweden and the United States we concluded
that consideration of energy use per unit of activity in these

countries suggests that we should be able to save considerable amounts of energy based on present Swedish energy-using techniques, mainly in the areas of automobiles (smaller), buildings (tighter), and industry (economies in the use of heat). However, this does not mean that Sweden is *better* at using energy than we are. Other countries show energy-saving methods that make even the best techniques in Sweden look wasteful.

The very concept of waste leans heavily on economics. The most notable difference in this respect in Sweden is the greater prices paid there for energy in all forms, with a few exceptions. It has simply made good economic sense to be more energy conserving there than here, as the table of energy prices (table 3) shows. This difference, in the view of a growing number of economists, social scientists, and technologists, is one important reason why Sweden uses energy more efficiently than we do. Yet there is no doubt that great flexibility exists in the need for energy in the long run, given economic stimuli to exploit that flexibility and policies that reinforce economies in the use of fuels and electricity. What can we learn from the Scandinavian experience?

Energy Lessons from Scandinavia

Certainly there is danger in presenting a simplified picture of energy use and conservation in other countries as we sort out our own prospects. Nevertheless, certain important lessons do emerge. First, and foremost, it is clear from the Swedish experience that we can live with higher priced energy if we use it more efficiently. Of course, the outcry against high prices in the United States reflects in part a genuine concern for the poor as well as a less than genuine longing to preserve the free lunch. That incomes and welfare amenities are far more evenly distributed in Scandinavia makes the issue of higher prices for energy far less likely to be front-page news there than in the United States, where any suggestion of a tax of five cents a gallon (less than one tenth of

Typical Prices Paid for Important Energy Forms in Sweden and the United States*

Energy type	United States				Sweden			
	1960	1970	1974	1970 (¢/kWh)	1960	1970	1974	1970 (¢/kWh)
Oil products (¢/gallon)								
Gasoline[a]	30	35	45	1.04	53	61	116	1.82
Diesel	23	28	35	0.83	42	48.8	90	1.45
Heating oil								
Small customers	15	18	35	0.50	13.3	13.2	40.6	0.37
Large customers	10.5	12	25	0.33				
Heavy oil	7	8	23	0.23	7	8.5	22.5	0.24
Gas (¢/MM Btu)								
Residential	82	87	113	0.29		550	680[b]	1.9
Industrial								
Firm Service	51	50		0.17				
Interruptable service	33	34		0.11				
Coal, industrial ($/ton)[c]	10	13	25	0.14		18		0.2
Electricity (¢/kWh)								
Base	2.75	2.75		2.75	3.14[e]	2.12[e]	2.3[d]	
Base and space heating	1.75	2.0		1.5		1.5	2.0[d]	
Industrial	1	1	1.5	0.4-2.1		0.93	1.8[d]	0.6-2.2

[a]Swedish gasoline taxes: 42¢ per gallon in 1970, about 68¢ per gallon in 1974. The U.S. prices include a tax of 10¢ to 13¢ per gallon. [b]Data for 1973. [c]Coal price excludes captive and utility coal. [d]Data for 1975. [e]Swedish figures are based on 1700 kWh/year (1960), 3000 kWh/year (1970), and 2000 kWh/year (1974).

*For more detailed references consult Schipper and Lichtenberg. Note that prices include taxes.

the current gasoline tax in Sweden) is grounds for a recall election. The response to the higher costs that these problems represent should be increased efficiencies of use brought about by the careful improvement of existing machines and structures and new ones. There should be an equally careful adjustment of lifestyles along voluntary lines, guided by, among other things, meaningfully higher costs for energy and its services. Indeed, this is the cornerstone of much of energy policy in Scandinavia, where less can be done to affect the supply of fuel than the use of it.

An additional lesson that comes from a consideration of energy in Scandinavia is that government has a potential role to play in the formation and maintenance of energy policies and measures. Indeed, government has long been active in the United States, subsidizing energy production, then later controlling the price of energy, building roads, supporting airports, and subsidizing the spread of suburbia. All of these factors tended to increase energy consumption. Unfortunately, the role of government usually is forgotten. Now it may be time for American governments, at all levels, to take an active part in promoting the saving of energy.

The Role of Government: Some Aspects of Swedish Energy Conservation Policy

One of the most important changes in energy policies that accompanied early conservation efforts was the tacit recognition that attention to the demand side of the energy problem was overdue and perhaps more rewarding than the preoccupation hitherto with its supply side. A few elements of the Swedish conservation program, suitably refined for American political tastes, are worth noting.

For one thing, taxes on energy are important if the price of energy today (even without controls and subsidies) is to represent all of society's costs of producing and using it. This was made clear in many of the expert reports to the Swedish Energy Commission in early 1978. With the possible exception of taxes on gas-guzzling cars, these taxes should be on fuels and electricity, not on other things relating to energy use.

Where private economic horizons and society's goals do not coincide, the government can help out by providing loans and subsidies for investment in conservation techniques. In Sweden nearly one billion dollars ($25 billion at U.S. population levels) has been provided in the form of loans and grants to homeowners, factories, apartments, and municipalities for the installation of energy-saving measures. An active propaganda campaign has provided information and exhortation to consumers. For the most part these investments ultimately displace larger investments elsewhere that would provide increments of energy supply. Careful statistical evaluation and follow-up of these programs is lacking. Only in factories have the results been unambiguously positive so far.

Building codes and efficiency standards help to stimulate these investments. (Such codes and standards will be increasingly important in the future.) The Swedish experience has not been completely without problems, but the building industry accepts the idea of codes because all entrepreneurs and potential buyers are affected thereby.

The speed of the political response to the need for energy policies, at least in Sweden, should not be glossed over. Sweden is a small country. Dissension over policy measures is easily overcome "within the family" as all political parties and interests strive for *samforstående*, or consensus. In the early days of the Swedish nuclear power debate, opposite sides always talked to each other. While the continuance of that debate does seem to be wearing everyone's patience thin, the degree of ease with which political consensus, and then action, is reached in Sweden remains striking. Only recently, as Lönnroth and his colleagues explain, have the political strains of the energy debate taken a serious toll.

Energy is not a new problem in Sweden. Swedish crown authorities were already beset with energy crises in the fourteenth and
eighteenth centuries as the cutting down of the forests for fire-
wood appeared to threaten the economy. The second of these
crises produced a remarkable invention, the Kakelugn (brick
furnace), a kind of indoor ceramic chimney, completely different
from our Franklin stove, which considerably increased the heat
obtained from burning wood or other fuels. In Denmark the
amount of wood needed to cook dropped measurably from the
fourteenth century until the beginning of the present epoch as
people discovered more efficient means of food preparation.

Energy and Society

With this picture of Swedish energy use in mind, the reader is
naturally curious about Swedish technologies that save energy.
While energy supply technologies are similar in the two countries,
our own work has turned up significant differences in various
end uses when the United States and Sweden are contrasted.
However, Lönnroth and his colleagues skip many of the technical
details without leaving any hint of antitechnological bias. They
have chosen to concentrate on social, political, and economic
factors that both *shape* energy development and, in turn, are
pushed and pulled by technology itself.

Why is this analysis of *Swedish* energy society relevant to read-
ers in other countries? First, the important links between cheap
energy and economic development in England and the United
States are well known; here the Swedish example is well documented. Second, Sweden has a high standard of living and a high
per capita (though efficient) energy use. Finally, the Swedish
debate over nuclear power, which became harsher after the April
1979 reactor incident in Harrisburg, Pennsylvania, has penetrated
political life so thoroughly as to make virtually every Swede
convinced *and* concerned about the energy problem.

It is, of course, often forcefully argued that Swedes, Americans, and Germans are so different politically, culturally, and socially, that comparisons of energy policies are not meaningful. Yet all countries face similar significant roadblocks to energy conservation and development. For this reason, the *Society* in *Energy and Society* must be examined as carefully as the *Energy*. This, of course, was the goal of the authors of *Energy in Transition*, a goal they achieved.

There are, of course, areas where ignorance of political differences are crucial. Community organization at the municipal level and land-use planning in Sweden, for example, have greatly aided the development of district heating. In the United States, by contrast, the political coherence that allows careful, long-range energy planning and cooperation seems to be lacking, at least at today's energy prices. Consequently the *social* variables that determine the acceptability (or adaptability) of a technology, often ignored, can be the most crucial of all. Moreover, new technologies have to win political battles, not just prove themselves technically and economically. Indeed, few engaged in the nuclear power debate question the *economic* calculations that accompany pleas for nuclear power. Instead nuclear power has been challenged largely for social and political reasons, reasons that may be perfectly legitimate.

The authors make an important point about economic and technical calculations. In the energy debate at large there are many claims as to the total direct and indirect costs of this policy or that. In their summary of "Solar Sweden," Lönnroth and his coauthors point out that the comparison of "Solar" and "Nuclear" Sweden becomes a wash economically: it would not be possible, or fair, to judge which future is cheaper to the degree of accuracy often claimed. This might be interpreted as a slap against the optimism expressed by backers of nearly every energy future, that is, those who claim that a particular path has certain-to-be-won benefits with well-determined costs. I do not interpret this to mean that economic calculations are no good, only that ultimately we may have to use political or social criteria because the economic evaluations neither ask nor answer all the important questions. However, Sydkraft, the southern Swedish private utility, placed an order for a substantial wind turbine system (5 megawatts) in late June of 1979. The political atmosphere of the nuclear debate in Sweden is doing just what my own reading of *Energy and Society* suggests—forcing society to take real steps with real technologies to see if the numbers might work out after all.

This new initiative for a utility presently operating nuclear plants is not surprising. Sweden, perhaps more than any other country with a substantial commitment to nuclear power, has come close to breaking that commitment. It is difficult at this writing to predict how nuclear power will fare when the fallout from Harrisburg settles. Basically, nuclear power in Sweden faces "Swedish" reassessment, inspired by the Harrisburg incident, a ballot initiative now called for in 1980, and the parliamentary elections of September 1979. I *personally* doubt whether the Swedes will vote to close existing nuclear power plants, but it appears at this time that they will most certainly tilt their own energy future away from any greater dependence upon this energy form and toward a greater use of solar heating and other forms of renewable energies. To lean purposefully away from nuclear power might be seen as foolhardy by some, brave by others. In a sense, other countries are fortunate that the Swedes seem nearest to taking a definite position. But the uncertainty over energy in transition in Sweden now makes a study of energy and society there more valuable than ever before.

Lawrence Berkeley Laboratory
1 July 1979

Data in all tables are taken from L. Schipper and A. Lichtenberg. *Science* 194 (3 Dec. 1976), 1001.

Introduction:
The Connecting Thread

ACCESS TO ENERGY is vital for our society. In the next few years our energy supplies will be based on fossil fuels (chiefly oil) and hydropower. However, oil production in the world may be expected to stagnate in perhaps fifteen to twenty-five years for resource availability reasons, or earlier for political and economic reasons. This means that oil must first be supplemented and later replaced by some other energy source, a situation that is discussed in chapter 2. Chapter 3 identifies the main alternatives: breeder reactors, coal, and renewable energy sources (e.g., solar energy in all its forms).

Because of the uncertainties attached to these alternatives technically, politically, economically, and environmentally, we should not take a final stand at this time on the choice of our future energy supply. On the contrary, we should take steps now to ensure freedom of action in that choice.

The alternatives possess varying characteristics: technical, economic, environmental, and organizational. Then, too, the supply of energy must fit into the pattern of energy use. All changes take a very long time to accomplish. That is why we discuss, in chapter 4, the risks of getting rigidly committed and the chances of maintaining and creating freedom of action, so that none of the alternatives disappears unintentionally.

Freedom of action has its limits, which lie mainly on three levels: the interaction of energy policy with other political goals; technical properties of the energy system; and characteristics of the economic and social system of rules among which the energy issues are to be found. These three levels are treated extensively in subsequent chapters.

Some conceivable conflicts over political goals are discussed in chapter 5, which takes up the relations between energy consumption on the one hand and economic growth, environmental protection, geographic structure, foreign policy, and so forth on the other.

Technical limits to freedom of action are the subject of chapter 6, which is chiefly concerned with the importance of energy quality and with energy carriers.

Organizational and institutional limits to freedom of action are discussed in chapter 7, taking as an example the development of the electricity sector in Sweden.

Chapter 8 traces the development of the nuclear program in Swedish energy policy, makes an attempt to assess the political situation, and describes a solar alternative.

1
Swedish Energy Policy: Today, Yesterday, Tomorrow

IN 1975 THE Swedish Parliament made a decision on energy policy which was concerned with the management of energy resources until 1985. The next decision of this kind was made in 1978, and was meant to shape the design of energy supply up to 1990.

A long series of investigations and studies has been set in motion to carry out the 1975 decision and to bring out source data for the 1978 decision. The Energy Research Delegation, the Energy Savings Committee, and the Energy Taxation Committee are among the investigating bodies. A new Energy Commission was appointed in December 1976.

The future study's role in this picture concentrates chiefly on farther-ranging issues, with discussion of how conditions and circumstances beyond, say, 1990 will affect those decisions that are going to be made in the next few years.

The 1975 decision on energy policy was made in light of various background factors, among them the OPEC oil embargo, the sharp increase in prices which followed, and a keenly waged debate on the pros and cons of nuclear power. This decision has also been seen as a milestone between two epochs: an outgoing epoch, where increasing supplies of energy went together with growing prosperity as a matter of course, and an incoming epoch, where energy supply per se is beginning to turn problematic, precarious, and bound up with negative consequences, which may prove substantial. It follows that the value of having energy in abundance must be weighed against the difficulties and conflicts

3

which arise when we try to ensure these energy quantities. It was at this crossroad that a policy of active energy management or husbandry was born, a policy which combines measures on the supply side with measures to hold back consumption.

A future study obviously must adopt a long-time perspective. But then the perspective should not only look ahead but backward, too. If future studies are going to be meaningful, reducing a complicated and multifaceted course of history into a few fundamental theses and nexuses becomes necessary in order to interpret the past as a basis for speculation on what might happen if we do this or that.

Many perils lurk here, of course. It is easy to take what is dramatic, and therefore of urgent moment, as a starting point for observations about the eternal laws, to extend the validity of the here and now to years and perhaps decades. It stands to reason that such "occupational hazards" cannot be overcome without intellectual rigor and unless critics can be counted on to blow their chill winds.

We think the adoption of a historical perspective toward energy policy can lower, at least, the risk of stumbling into certain pitfalls. As part of the project framework, therefore, a fairly large volume of work has been devoted to understanding Swedish energy policy since the end of the nineteenth century as a springboard for understanding its dictates over the rest of the twentieth century. Although this review will be documented more completely later on, here we review some of its main features in the present context.

The concept "energy policy" is fairly new in the political process. For long periods Sweden used to have a wood policy, a coal policy, and an electricity policy. Wood policy formed one part of forest policy, since the woodlands comprised a resource with several applications. Coal policy was bound up with foreign policy, and so on.

By and by the once separate policies pursued with regard to wood, coal, peat, and other nonrenewable energy sources, coalesced into a single fuel policy in the early 1950s; the electricity and fuel policies were combined during the 1950s into one energy policy.

One reason seems to be that the markets for electric power and fuels gradually overlapped one another. To illustrate, electricity for heating purposes became feasible in an area where fuels used to dominate. Another reason seems to be that certain technical systems offered opportunities for producing electricity and/or district heating, namely nuclear power and back pressure (the combined generation of electricity and hot water for district heating).

One of the conclusions to be drawn from the foregoing is that it is not at all axiomatic that in the future we will retain energy as a concept which embodies an entire field of political discourse. New technical systems may link parts of the energy question with totally different political issues. Among other things, organizational design is partly governed by such factors.

Swedish energy use since the beginning of the twentieth century chiefly relates to fuels, whereas energy policy is concerned with electricity for the most part. By far the greater part of central government's investigative and decision-making capacity has been devoted to that part of the energy balance accounted for by electricity, which, though limited in volume, requires heavy capital investment. Even this simple observation conceals, we think, an important aspect of energy policy: namely, that the transition from wood to coal, from coal to oil, and so forth, took place almost entirely under rules pertinent to the market economy, and hence within the framework of existing legislation. By contrast, introducing and developing electricity has required never-ending legislative labors, that is, a continuous adjustment of role allocation or of the prevailing division of responsibilities to the demands of a new technology. Having said this, we have also said that the chances of introducing new energy technologies simply and painlessly very much depend on what today's institutional conditions look like.

These conditions are adapted in their turn to existing energy technologies.

The concept "energy conservation" is not new. It cropped up as far back as the eighteenth century, when the authorities were worried seriously about the wood supply, and received its most concrete expression with the introduction of a heating device that was sparing of fuel: the upright porcelain stove. The idea surfaced anew with the 1951 Fuels Commission in a report that saw active energy-saving efforts as the best way to overcome a threatening overdependence on oil. At that time the avowed intention was to encourage the insulation of dwellings, to develop wind power, heat pumps, and other modes of fuel husbandry.

By the time the Fuels Commission published its final report in 1956, all thoughts of pursuing an active conservation policy had been forgotten. The dependence on imports would not be solved by the exercise of restraint on the user side but by resort to nuclear power, that is, with measures on the supply side. One wonders what the situation might have been in 1975 if all the exertions and resources expended over the past twenty years on developing new supply systems had been expended instead on the user side.

We can only speculate on why the mood shifted from 1951 to 1956. One reason, certainly, was the emergence of domestic nuclear power as an alternative to oil. In the late 1940s, moreover, the giant oil fields in the Middle East began to produce in volume, which brought gradually falling oil prices in its train. Another reason, presumably, was that an active policy of energy conservation is simply much more complicated to administer than an active policy for increasing the supply. In other respects, too, the 1950s brought an upswing in confidence in the market economy as a self-adjusting mechanism and the posture of deploring administrative interference and governmental regulation.

Many crucial decisions on development of the energy supply system are made by people other than members of Parliament and Cabinet, that is, the legislative and executive branches of government. As shown by the studies we have made of the growth of the Swedish energy supply system, decisions which sometimes have crucially affected the course of events have been made outside (or rather below) the political level in society. Such decisions may have to do with rate structures, satisfaction of engineering criteria, forms of collaboration and joint ventures between, say, the producers of electrical power and its distributors. Trade associations and professional groups apparently play big roles. To all intents and purposes, therefore, the practical scope for assigning political accountability for the structure of the energy supply system is very limited indeed.

Accordingly, we think we can establish that the energy sector's technical design depends greatly on the organizational division of responsibilities that has prevailed and still prevails by and large. This role allocation holds not only between private firms and society but also, and perhaps above all, among different parts of the public administration—centrally/regionally/locally—between producers and distributors, between experts/professional groups and the political level, and so on.

Now what conclusions can we draw from these historical observations?

Up until the 1970s a good energy policy was one that provided the community at large with the cheapest energy possible.

Energy was seen as one of the cornerstones on which to build a growing prosperity. The only perceived threat was to our national security, which might be jeopardized if imports were cut off.

The supply of energy is still a cornerstone which underpins our material well-being. And it is still necessary to guard ourselves as far as possible against the consequences of a blockade situation. So on these counts no changes actually have occurred. But in addition the energy supply sector is beginning to give rise to other negative consequences which are growing. Cases in point are the pollution of the environment, the availability of fossil fuels in the long run, the effects of our dependence on the outside world, and perhaps, too, organizational institutional consequences. How does one retain political control over an increasingly important technocracy?

In such a situation it is no longer just as easy to say what makes a good energy policy in general and what energy source is worth backing in particular. Uncertainty has grown visibly and, if anything, keeps right on growing.

The political expression of this uncertainty in the 1975 decision on energy policy put stress on the concept "freedom of action." It boils down to this: we don't want to become prisoners of the energy system and be forced to make decisions where real alternatives are lacking. In other words, freedom of action is an instrument for obtaining a good energy supply system. But like all instruments it calls for sacrifices: economic, intellectual, and emotional. Freedom of action won't be ours for the taking; at the same time it may well turn out to be a highly justified insurance premium.

The emphasis on striking a balance between demand and supply of energy and the desire to create freedom of action are bound to change the dictates of energy policy in other respects as well.

Until now the choice among energy sources has been struck in all essentials by the professional groups—engineers and other experts—who work within the energy sector. Hence it is at this level of society that energy policy has so far been devised in practice. The political level, above all Cabinet and Parliament, has played a more central role only by way of exception.

The demand for increased freedom of action in the choice among future energy sources will necessitate another division of responsibilities between the political and technical levels.

This report seeks to discuss the terms which we consider applicable to a policy of greater freedom of action in the choice of energy supply systems.

2
Getting Away from Today's Energy Systems

Introduction

SWEDEN WAS NOT the only country to start discussing energy policy for the long term after what happened in 1973 on the oil market. The need for more and more energy to fuel sustained economic growth was measured against various prophecies about limited resources, especially of oil and gas but also of uranium. In this chapter we shall present some data on global energy supply and try to draw some conclusions for Sweden.

The Flow of Energy on Earth

An even flow of energy comes to earth from the sun. This keeps the earth's temperature above that in cold outer space, propels currents in the atmosphere and oceans, imparts motion to the water cycle and generates photosynthesis in plants. Figure 1, which illustrates these energy flows on earth, also shows the energy that is converted by society through the markets for energy of different forms. The global flows in the figure have been expressed as multiples of the amount that is converted by society. For instance, it will be seen that photosynthesis converts eight times as much energy as society does, that the amount of energy radiated to earth from the sun is 30,000 times that which society converts. Most of the energy for society appears to come from fossil fuels, which are renewed at a negligibly slow rate by means of anaerobic breakdown processes. The fossil fuels strongly dominate society's energy supply; their proportion amounts to about 85 percent.

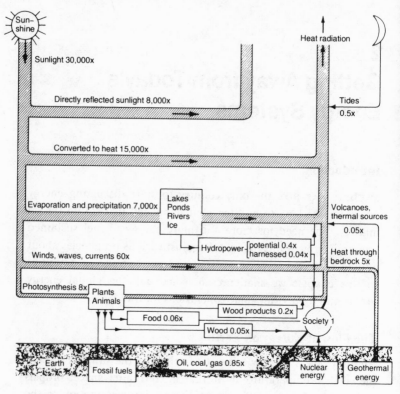

Fig. 1. Energy flow on earth. The energy flows are standardized to energy conversion by society, which is set at 1 (one).

We thus assimilate both the natural energy flow and the energy flow created by man in the industrialized system. Although the former is overwhelmingly dominant in size, some of its characteristics fit poorly into present-day patterns of energy use. The latter flow is much smaller but has evolved together with the user side and therefore now makes a good fit with that side. If somehow we can cleverly exploit the natural energy flow for what we regard as necessary energy uses, the quantity of energy apparently poses no problem—that's how large this flow is.

Given this general background, we would like to make three distinctions which we think necessary:

Renewable/finite energy sources are a frequently used basis of classification. Later on in this report we shall account at greater length for what we now know abut finite sources.

Quantity/quality. Energy flows are described in terms of MWh (megawatt hour) or the like. One then disregards the fact that, say, 1 MWh of electricity is more useful than 1 MWh of oil, which in its turn is more useful than 1 MWh in the form of 100°C hot water. The quality concept has to do with usefulness, and one cardinal reason why stored energy sources are used so much lies precisely in their high quality. Roughly speaking, one can say that there is plenty of low-quality energy and less and less high-quality energy. At the same time we must have energy of high quality for certain applications. We return to this problem in chapter 4: ("What types of energy do we need?").

Commercial/noncommercial energy. Certain energy forms have commercial value today while others do not. This point is important because the statistics on energy use are usually based on what has been sold, not what is actually used. For instance, much of the energy requirement in developing countries is met by wood or dung, which is gathered locally and as such is never recorded in the energy budgets. In an industrialized nation like Sweden, we assimilate insolation (solar energy) through the windows that face south on our houses, which are also heated with the electricity that reaches the radiators via the electric-power line. But we count no more than the electricity. These factors have great bearing upon any discussion of what one is really supposed to mean by speaking of zero growth in the energy use. (An interesting analogy is to be found here with the conceptual pair, work/employment. Only the hours of work that are sold on the market are termed "employment.")

Society, Energy Use, and Welfare

Back in 1850 a Swede would consume annually energy roughly equivalent to about 0.3 tons of oil (3.5 MWh). Energy sources then were wood, which he or his family gathered, coal and coke, and muscle power from human beings and animals. In 1973 his descendants used energy equivalent to about 4.7 tons (55 MWh) per person per year. It was brought in the form of oil or electricity and used for personal consumption (home heating, driving the family car) or to manufacture consumer products.

The change since 1850 does not pertain to energy use alone. Sweden achieved its industrialization and high standard of living because the once so self-supporting peasant or crofter entered the factories, where he produced not only for his own needs but also for those of others. An accumulation of capital carried to ever greater lengths, combined with the division of labor, made possible increased production and with that growing prosperity.

But increased production presupposed a changed structure of urban settlements and with them a changed residential pattern. The necessary division of labor presupposed in its turn an ever greater input of coordination—both in production and in consumption. These demands have in their turn put new demands on production, for instance, of transport equipment and time-saving domestic appliances.

There is no doubt that increasing energy use has been necessary for increased prosperity. As far as it goes, one could imagine building up a society without one or the other raw material, but one could never imagine a society—or indeed any kind of activity —without energy.

Actually, the fact that energy plays such a fundamental role for developing society only makes it harder to analyze what the connections look like.

We can obtain certain insights, admittedly anecdotal for the most part, by comparing ouselves with other cultures. A society in which the only energy source is human labor (via photosynthesis) has very great limitations in social organization. Even the introduction of draft animals serves to increase the efficiency of conversion from solar energy (photosynthesis) to mechanical work, which can then be used to build up the society. More food can be produced per person, the prerequisites increase for an incipient specialization and hence for a more complex culture.

When we later add an energy converter like the sailing ship (conversion of solar energy via wind energy to kinetic energy) even more opportunities for specializing are put in hand, which favors the growth of trading patterns. The advent of the steam engine in the eighteenth century made additional surplus energy available.

Another example of what energy technology means for social organization can be taken from medieval England. The transition from oxen to horses in agriculture can be seen in this context as a case of increased efficiency in the conversion of solar energy (via photosynthesis) to mechanical work: the horse worked faster than the ox. As a result agricultural productivity went up, dwellings could be sited farther from the fields, and the transition from dispersed to concentrated (village) settlement was encouraged. All these things in their turn affected the entire organization of English society.

In our time it is evident that the supply of cheap and easily transported energy, say in the form of oil and electricity, has had a fundamental bearing upon the growth of the transport apparatus and, concomitantly, residential patterns and specialized production. Economic historians often point up the importance of railway construction for the nineteenth century and, by the same token, of automobile usage for the twentieth century.

For present purposes let us just observe that the terms of future energy policy will be determined largely by what material level of living we want to have and what we want our everyday life—our life style—to look like. This is a topic we shall pursue at greater length. First we are going to discuss which energy sources society utilizes.

Society's Energy Sources

The world's energy supply comes mainly from fossil fuels.

TABLE 1
ENERGY FORMS

	%	Mtoe
Oil	49	2,840
Coal	30	1,740
Natural gas	18	1,060
Hydropower	1.9	
Nuclear power	0.9	

In 1973 the global energy conversion amounted to 5,800 Mtoe (67,000 TWh) distributed by energy forms as above. Heavy dependence on these fuels stands out clearly. Table 2 sets out known reserves of fossil fuels and uranium. The term *reserves* refers to known deposits in the earth's crust which can be recovered with known technology at current prices. Over and above these reserves, of course, there are assets of various fuels as yet unidentified. Just how large these quantities are has been the subject of much speculation (we shall come back to them in a moment). The reserves comprise one part of the resources of, say, oil. It follows that *resources* refers to total deposits, including those which are not accessible with known technology or at competitive prices but which are deemed to become accessible with new technology and higher prices, including deposits of sorts not yet identified. So with new technology and higher prices some resources pass over into reserves. It should be pointed out that we know very little about how the amount of reserves increases when prices rise.

It will be seen from table 2 that coal is abundant and that reserves of coal, assuming the rates of use in 1973, equal 200 years of consumption, while the corresponding numbers of years are 33 for oil and 43 for gas. The estimated resources of coal exceed the reserves here reported by a factor of about twenty. So there will be no limitations on the availability of coal during the next two centuries or more for geological reasons.

As noted, oil accounts for a preponderance of the world's energy supply. Several methods have been used to evaluate the resources of oil in the earth's crust. Estimates cluster around 250,000 Mtons (millions of tons), with a minimum of 170,000 Mtons at one extreme and a maximum of 340,000 Mtons at the other. Whichever estimate we accept, the fact remains that oil must be regarded as a finite asset. With today's consumption and a resource amount of 250,000 Mtons, it would "suffice" for about 100 years; with consumption going up at the rate prevailing in the 1960s, it would "suffice" for 25 years (figure 2).

To state that reserves and resources "suffice" is to indulge in inexactitude. Nor is sufficiency the concept which interests us. Instead, let us discuss that point in time when oil production is likely to stagnate. It is at this point that we must have alternatives at hand which can gradually replace the stagnating and eventually diminishing oil output. The alternatives may be other energy sources or more efficient energy use.

Figure 3 shows the historical trend for annual oil production in the world, the reserves remaining after each year, and the changing ratio of these reserves to annual output. It will be seen that output has risen rapidly in the past twenty years and that reserves have likewise increased sharply, thanks to successful exploration. From around 1950, however, the ratio between them has steadily fallen.

But this ratio between reserves and production cannot go lower than between 10 or 15, because physical constraints impose upper limits on the pace at which oil can be recovered from a field, which means there must be a residual amount of oil in every field in the course of extraction. Besides, it takes time before new fields can be made to produce. As the era of oil on earth draws to a

TABLE 2
PROVEN RESERVES OF STORED ENERGY FORMS

	Fossil fuels, in Mtoe					Nuclear fuel in TWh	
	Solid fuels	Crude oil	Gas	Oil shale, tar sands	Total	Uranium, thermal reactors	Uranium and thorium, breeder reactors
Africa	9,100	13,300	5,100	2,000	29,500	58,100	3,490,000
Asia, total (excl. Soviet Union)	65,700	55,700	10,900	21,600	153,900	900	55,000
Middle East	700	42,700	3,700	—	47,100	200	11,000
China	56,000	1,800	600	21,600	80,000	unknown	unknown
Japan	800	—	—	—	800	700	44,000
Europe, total (excl. Soviet Union)	61,600	1,400	3,900	2,900	69,800	14,000	2,700,000
Eastern Europe	27,000	400	400	—	27,800	unknown	unknown
rest of Europe	34,600	1,000	3,500	2,900	42,000	14,000	2,700,000
Soviet Union	83,800	8,400	14,600	3,500	110,300	unknown	unknown
North America	127,800	7,600	9,600	229,500	374,500	124,000	9,325,000
United States	124,200	5,800	6,800	152,000	288,800	78,900	5,485,000
Canada	3,200	1,100	2,300	77,500	84,100	44,600	3,822,000
South America	1,300	7,800	1,500	600	11,200	3,500	1,045,000
Australia and rest of Oceania	11,600	200	600	200	12,600	29,000	1,742,000
Total (rounded off)	361,000	95,000	46,000	260,000	762,000	299,000	18,400,000
Total expressed in thousand TWh							

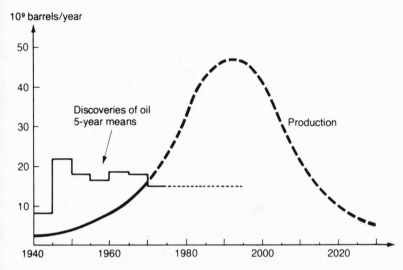

Fig. 2. The world's future oil production if recovery continues to rise each year by 7.5 percent, as happened in 1950-1970, and the total reserves are 270,000 million tons. Note that the annual discoveries will soon fall short of the annual output. A lower rate of production increase will delay the onset of stagnation.

close, the ratio of reserves to production will fall. In other words, new deposits will have to be found at an ever faster rate to keep overall output from stagnating. Production in 1975 totaled 2,700 Mtons, which was down from the 1974 level. The size of new finds that will have to be made come to 2,500—5,000 Mtons per annum. For the sake of comparison, four previously unknown areas have been discovered since the late 1950s: the North Sea (2,700 Mtons), Alaska (1,500 Mtons), Nigeria (3,400 Mtons), and Libya (4,700 Mtons). Reserves have been increased otherwise by discoveries and by upgrading estimates in previously known areas.

A number of factors will affect that point in time when oil production stagnates. Physical-geological properties are one class of factors; technological advance, political and economic conditions are others. The relations between oil companies and oil-exporting countries have become more and more complicated

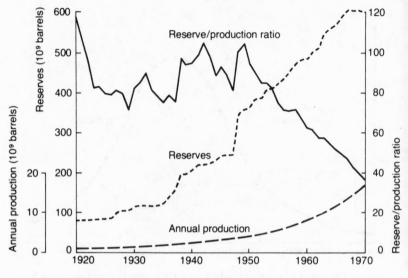

Fig. 3. World production of oil, remaining reserves, and ratio of reserves to production during the period 1920–1970. The unit for reserves and production is 10^9 barrels, equivalent to 140 Mtoe.

(see chapter 3: "The transition of time perspective, mechanisms, and distribution of powers"), which also tends toward an early stagnation date.

According to a widely held view, the United States reached its production peak in 1970. A similar prediction for the world as a whole puts the peak anywhere from 1985 to 1995. Other predictions lie in the time interval 1990–2000.

The big question, of course, is whether alternatives to oil will then be available or whether energy use must adapt to the finite supply of oil.

We shall return to this matter, but here we emphasize that the point is not to guess the stagnation date correctly but rather to try to understand how various oil producers and consumers will act, both on the national and international stage, when they become increasingly uncertain about the long-term availability of cheap-to-produce oil.

For natural gas the uncertainty concerning total resources is greater than for oil. Some estimates speak of reserves twice as great as those in table 2, others of much higher values. Gas is incompletely utilized at the present time and huge quantities are allowed to burn off in the oil-production process because there is no ready market. One reason for this is that gas is much more expensive to transport than oil (per unit of energy).[1] If major gas reserves exist, large parts of them probably lie in inaccessible tracts in Siberia, with accompanying problems of economically viable exploitation.

Even so, it is not impossible that gas can play a role as an adjunct to oil for a limited period and in certain regions. To illustrate for Western Europe, gas is obtainable from no less than four sources: the North Sea, the Middle East, North Africa, and the Soviet Union. Heavy capital investment is necessary, however, and the foreign policy complications are obvious.

Oil shales and tar sands are also shown in table 2. Enormous amounts of energy are bound in these forms, but the difficulties of extracting them on a large scale are great. Although the total supply is of very doubtful certainty, large-scale deposits exist in countries like Canada and Venezuela. The capital outlays will be immense and so will be the need for other resources, such as water. It is not impossible that limits will be set not so much by the strictly economic criteria as by the environmental and, perhaps, by the social consequences of the very large interventions required if these energy forms are really going to have any importance for the world's energy balance. Put differently: the economy and hence the price of energy to its consumers will depend largely on the considerations those consumers are prepared to take for the environment and the social structure in regions where the deposits exist. So apart from technical problems, there are clearcut political problems which may impede exploitation.

1. Relative costs of transmitting a given amount of energy over a certain distance are 1 for an oil pipeline, 2.5 for a gas pipeline, 5.5 for train-hauled coal, and 17 for a 500 kV electric power line.

Similar problems apply to nuclear power, especially as reflected by the current technological emphasis on the light-water reactors. The uranium reserves now recoverable at a price of US $30/pound are equivalent to 3 percent of the energy contained in estimated oil resources. Uranium exploration has been considerably more restricted than the search for oil, and it is not at all unreasonable to expect that large amounts of uranium will be found in the future. As for the very large amounts of uranium to be found in extremely low-grade ores, the environmental and social consequences of producing uranium on a large scale presumably will set the upper limits (or at all events create conflicts). Where ore contents are very low, there also arises the question of whether the energy that can be produced from them is great enough to cover the energy required for extraction.

Seen globally, therefore, it is unlikely that nuclear power—given today's reactor technology—can replace oil. On the other hand it can become a complement.

Accordingly we may summarize global energy supplies as follows. Oil that is cheap to produce is nearing the end of its days. That goes for cheap natural gas as well. These energy forms must first be supplemented and later wholly replaced by other energy sources. This is the observation we have taken as our fundamental postulate for the future study. Just as when coal once took over from wood and oil from coal, we stand on the threshold of a transitional period.

3
Toward Tomorrow's Energy Systems

Historical Transition of Energy Sources

FIGURE 4 SHOWS how different types of energy have superseded one another in Sweden.

Wood as a dominant energy source first gave way to coal and coke, which together reached a share of about 50 percent at the beginning of the twentieth century. Oil was introduced into Sweden during the same period and has mostly replaced both wood and coal. Hydropower has grown to a stable level, while nuclear power is now beginning to carve out a noticeable share in our energy balance.

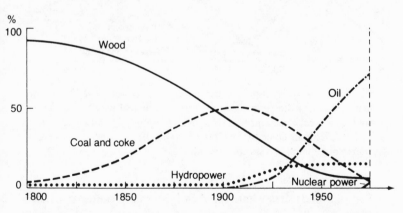

Fig. 4. Shares of various energy types in Sweden's energy supply, 1800–1975.

Obviously, these changes have both presupposed and impelled changes in both the technical and organizational systems in which the energy supply is included. For instance, wood was partly used for heating by individual consumers in their fireplaces. The transition from wood to coal for heating purposes was partly bound up with the transition from open fires to central heating (circulating hot water and boilers). This permitted the later transition from coal to oil and from central heating to district heating.

A look at energy supply in the United States gives us the following picture.

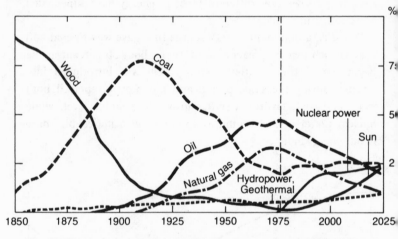

Fig. 5. USA's energy supply from different sources during 1850–1975 and a projection to the year 2020. In this hypothetical scenario six energy sources will each account for less than 25 percent of USA's energy supply in 2020. This in contrast to the past when, as in Sweden, one energy source dominated in a specific period.

Figure 5 illustrates what is known from many contexts: it takes a very long time for an energy source to gain or lose a large market share. Thirty to forty years have been needed to move up from a market share of 10 percent to 25 percent.

Naturally, the length of the time period is due to the fact that new energy sources always require new technology and new investments, new competence, and new ways of working together. Existing equipment, knowledge, and organizational forms constitute real capital that cannot be replaced overnight without incurring heavy macroeconomic losses. We have no reason to suppose that these lead times have become shorter with the years nor to expect that the pace of change is going to be substantially different in the future, unless one feels compelled to go in for some sort of "crash program." The implementation of such programs can be a comparatively speedy process, but then it is more valid to speak of different "catastrophe scenarios" that would bring drastic and costly changes in their train.

There is another lesson to be learned from this picture of the United States. Oil did not supersede coal because coal "ran out" but because oil was simpler and cheaper to handle and transport, and permitted new types of machinery. In other words oil replaced coal because it cut down on energy prices.

This is not self-evident but a consequence of technological development. An ever greater part of the energy contained in coal is transported in the form of electricity, which is one method of cheapening the use of, say, coal. The development of coal technology was thought to have ground to a halt for several decades, but now huge sums of money are being invested in advancing this technology.

On the whole it is necessary to put the observed transitions from one energy source to another into technical, economic, and institutional perspective.

Accordingly we can establish that the transition from one energy source to another is not new. Society has switched bases before. What is new is that we are no longer going to get falling prices for energy. On the contrary, off-shore oil now costs between 10 and 100 times as much to extract as oil from the giant fields of the Middle East (where the production cost is below Skr 5/m^3); on a rough estimate, synthetic liquid fuels from coal and oil shale now cost twice as much to produce (about Skr 600–700/m^3) as the current oil price, not counting energy tax. As far as we can see today, many future energy sources will be more expensive than today's oil.

Moreover, the energy system is getting to be so important and interwoven with other social sectors that a decision to switch sources obviously cannot be left either to anonymous market forces or to a technological imperative ("if you can, you must"). Today, there are brand new criteria for laying down the procedure and decision-making process to be used to pick out the next array of energy sources. In short, the mechanisms governing the transition have changed.

Conceivable Future Energy Sources

The outlooks for adding to and then gradually replacing the two cheap sources, oil and natural gas, can be regarded in two time perspectives.

The *first time perspective* takes in the next ten to twenty years and as such presumably includes the point in time when oil production is due to stagnate. In this time perspective the only technologies that can play any quantitative role are those which are either in commercial operation today or nearly so. We are already familiar with all the essentials of these technologies; it is the speed with which they can be introduced where most of the doubts come in.

The *second time perspective* is more remote and also contains technologies of the kind which are now found in the research and/or development stage. Here the uncertainty is much greater of course, but we still know enough to be able to draw some qualitative conclusions. The composition of the economy plays a big role in this longer time frame.

In all essentials there are three main sources for future energy supply:

Nuclear power. Only in the first time perspective is today's nuclear power technology available. It consists chiefly of non-breeder reactors (i.e., reactors which do not draw to any more significant extent on the most abundant uranium isotope, U-238). Most of these reactors are of the light-water reactor type (LWR). The world's uranium deposits are so limited that present-day nuclear power technology should be seen only as an adjunct to oil. They can scarcely be a substitute.

In the second time perspective are the breeder reactors (mainly of the liquid-metal fast breeder reactor type, LMFBR), which make much more efficient use of uranium. Theoretically, the breeder reactor could provide us with enormous amounts of energy in the future. A strong argument for the breeder reactor is that it is a natural continuation of today's commitment to nuclear power. The industry itself has looked upon the breeder reactor as such ever since the 1950s. Moreover, huge sums have been and are being spent on its development. It has yet to evolve into a full-fledged technique for industrial use, and it is still far from certain that this reactor type can be developed into a workable and acceptable energy supply alternative. The reactors are available on demonstration scale, while the necessary reprocessing plants (which are not identical with those now being planned for the light-water reactors) are at the research stage. Breeder reactors presuppose plutonium handling on a big scale, a prospect fraught with risks of the proliferation of nuclear weapons, terrorism, and hazardous working environments. Breeder reactors would otherwise fit rather naturally into present-day systems of electric power generation. The only question is: at what cost, in terms of safety, economic viability, and social organization?

Coal and heavy oils. As noted earlier, there are huge amounts of coal in the earth's crust. And since coal has been used for a long time, a technology has developed to deal with it. For instance, coal is now the world's leading source of energy for electricity generation.

Sweden, which once used a great deal of coal, is virtually lacking in indigenous coal deposits, in addition to which it has no facilities for large-scale coal handling (such as transport systems and stockpiles). In the first time perspective coal is nevertheless an alternative for Sweden, this time using today's technology—direct combustion. Coal, too, comes with considerable problems in the first time perspective. A number of contaminants such as sulfur, heavy metals, and nitrogen oxides are important during this time perspective, together with the foreign policy complications mentioned earlier.

The second time perspective enlarges the technological options. Intense research is now going into different ways and means of producing liquid and gaseous fuels from coal. The heavy oils, which for example are to be found in tar sands, also may become feedstocks for the manufacture of synthetic fuels.

It is still too early to say whether synthetic fuels can supersede today's oil and natural gas. In any event the costs will be enormous, and no small part of them will depend necessarily on what ecological and social consequences we are willing to accept.

In the longer time perspective the use of coal and heavy oils may be restricted by the atmosphere's carbon dioxide content, which is increasing on account of combustion. If this increase is shown to have a highly deleterious effect on the earth's climate—a fear voiced by some scientists—the use of coal will have to be restricted, in which case it will not offer a main alternative for the world's energy supply.

Even a large-scale commitment to new coal technologies would have considerable consequences for social organization. The capital requirements will be enormous, and the environmental consequences would presumably be of similar magnitude.

Renewable energy sources. The annual insolation falling on Sweden's surface area is about 500,000 TWh (about 1 TWh/km^2), that is, more than 1,000 times greater than Sweden's energy balance. We already tap one variant of solar energy, hydropower, to produce about 80 percent of our electric energy (or about 15 percent of our total energy use). So it is not the amount of flowing energy which primarily limits our utilization of insolation. If anything, the problems are created by factors such as the low intensity of insolation (approximately 100 W/m^2 of mean power over the year) and its distribution over time. If we are going to tap the renewable energy sources, a cardinal question for us to answer will be how to arrange our energy system, from collection to use, so as to enable us to deflect and assimilate this flow in some clever fashion. A straightforward example: not quite half of all energy use in Sweden goes for space heating. Each year the roof of a single-family, detached house receives from five to ten times as much solar energy as is needed to heat the house. Simple strategems can be used to tap parts of this flow, as exemplified by windows facing south (plus thermostat) and solar collectors (plus heat storage). Even now nearly full-fledged technology is commercially available for the first time perspective, above all to engage the sun's warmth for space heating but also to harness wind power for electricity generation. Furthermore, the first time perspective can accommodate techniques like pyrolysis to recover, say, methane from organic material such as biomass or solid waste. Heat pumps for the earth's surface warmth can also be put into this category. Taken together these techniques represent a not unimportant potential for the first time perspective.

In the second perspective the uncertainties are obviously greater, but so are the possibilities. A facility is already in hand for converting sunlight to electricity via photocells, for example, but the costs are now immense. New possibilities would open up if these costs were to drop sharply thanks to mass production. Other variants combine the production of electricity and heat from sunlight. Together with cheap fuel cells driven by, say, hydrogen, one can imagine new ways of combining such future energy techniques. An apparently promising development is offered by plants specifically cultivated to convert, at a high rate of efficiency, insolation to organic matter (biomass). According to recent reports, moreover, selected plant species can produce petroleum directly. Energy forests can play an important role (see chapter 5: "Energy and geographic structure"). Biomass can be used through direct combustion for electricity and heat generation or to produce a fuel like methanol. In addition there are possibilities of combining energy production with sewage and waste management. All things considered, the renewable energy sources represent a rich variety in the longer time perspective. However, the uncertainties are very great indeed. Finally, it should be pointed out that these techniques will probably differ from today's energy systems in that they will demand changed social relations.

Over the very long term there are other possibilities. Fusion might well become technically feasible, but the principle has yet to be demonstrated and immense engineering problems can be foreseen. If the earth's magma can be effectively tapped for its heat, geothermal energy could provide another very big energy resource. Here again no technology has been made likely beyond some local use, and for the same reason: the knowledge base is deficient. We do not discuss fusion and geothermal energy as alternatives but rather look upon them as contingencies, for which the uncertainties are too great to permit their inclusion in a planning system. Further research for the rest of this century will probably yield a better ground on which to assess their possibilities.

For Sweden the situation is very much like that of the major industrial countries because of the heavy import requirement. This requirement varies widely, however, and we differ from many other countries in that we are totally lacking in oil, gas, and coal. We are heavily dependent on the industrial countries technically, economically, and culturally. Even so, we do have some advantages. In 1975, as noted, hydropower gave us about 80 percent of our electric power (and about 15 percent of Sweden's total energy use). We have uranium in Billingen equivalent to about 2,000 years of reactor operation (LWR), which equals 10,000 TWh or 25 years of energy use at the 1975 level. Native deposits of peat can supply energy for about 100 years of use. However, the exploitation of these resources is beset with difficulties. The peat covers about 12 percent of the country's area and mining it would work great changes on the land, not only where the peat bogs are located. Uranium extraction also leads to great land changes and other environmental problems. In our opinion, therefore, they cannot form the backbone of a Swedish energy supply system for any longer period. All the same, they could still contribute to our energy supply during a transitional phase.

Summarizing: the transition away from oil should be regarded in two time perspectives. During the first, oil production in the world will stagnate, and with it Swedish oil imports as well. This is likely to happen within the next twenty-five years, during which oil will have to be supplemented and, later, gradually replaced.

The second time period can be described roughly by saying that synthetic fuels will perhaps play a big role then. Supplies of oil (and natural gas) are limited. The new techniques then coming to the fore will embody coal and perhaps tar sands and oil shale, nuclear power and renewable sources. Energy-saving measures are still important, but so will be the question of the economy's composition.

From here on the discussion will be about the decision-making process. Restated in question form: Where are developments headed, and to what extent can we here in Sweden choose an energy future?

The Transition: Time Perspective, Mechanisms, and Distribution of Powers

What is the next transition going to look like? What are the mechanisms that will control the changeover? In this section we shall discuss various ways of thinking about international energy supply and present some conclusions for Sweden. Two interpretations of future transition can be said to oppose one another.

Both are interpretations of global development as it unfolded in recent years.

The first signifies that the next transition will move along essentially the same track as its predecessors. True, we did run into snags between 1970 and 1975, but these were chance occurrences and do not represent any fundamental difficulties. Technological advance and market forces can safely be counted on to make for a development that is largely smooth and problem-free.

According to the second interpretation, the difficulties of recent years are indeed fundamental and as such are symptoms of problems that lie deeper, problems with consequences for growth in environment and social relations, in deciding on technological alternatives, in making allocations globally and nationally, not to mention linking these difficulties to the necessary provision of energy, food, water, land, housing, and for a growing population.

It might be asked whether it is at all possible to decide which interpretation is the right one. The choice depends far too much on how one perceives the society and bears crucially on the conclusions that are drawn about future energy policy and, above all, about the roles of national governments.

The first interpretation gives national governments an essentially supporting role when it comes to research and development, enforcing the ground rules of the market economy nationally and internationally, guaranteeing the investment climate, acting as risk-bearer of last resort.

The second interpretation gives national governments a much more conflicted role. They are called on to support some but oppose other powerful interest groups, to uphold the existing economic world order and yet to improve it.

These distinctions are important since national governments will play an ever bigger role in relation to future energy technology. Earlier (in chapter 1) we called attention to the distinct roles played by the state when oil and hydropower were introduced into Sweden. Every new energy source will require some sort of contribution from the state—but there is a great difference from one source to another.

We shall elaborate on these perceptions in chapter 7 and here simply point out that the key roles of the state and public administration are important for understanding the transition mechanisms.

As we have seen in chapter 2, the date for a scarcity-dictated stagnation of the conventional petroleum output may not be farther away than ten to twenty-five years from now. This allows for what is now deemed to be a reasonable rate of advancing technology.

The time picture is also affected by political factors. Most of the geographic areas which look promising for oil exploration are to be found in developing countries but the economic world order is not presently conducive to any significant exploration efforts in those developing countries.

Exploration incurs great costs. Successful exploration is also supposed to finance the failures. So far the oil companies have performed this function of "risk-spreader," and as such have used (part of) the profits from one country to cover the losses in another. From the point of view of the oil companies, this is a reasonable course of action. But seen from the country where oil was discovered, another picture emerges. Why should that country allow the oil company to take out more money than is necessary to meet the company's real costs?

Threats of nationalization and control of profits suggest to many companies that they explore in "safer" areas. But this can also put the individual governments under pressure to secure more and more promising areas. Perhaps some international organization can provide an umbrella under whose protection governments and companies can work in harmony.

It follows that if energy resources are going to be available, substantial economic resources will have to be committed to those places where the reserves are located, otherwise production may stagnate for economic-political reasons.

But even if oil production is maintained at a high level, it cannot be taken for granted that Sweden will be able to import the quantities it would like. For instance, the access of industrial countries to oil produced in the developing world may decline because of a collapse and regionalization of the prevailing international oil economy. Of the petroleum reserves that are known today, the developing countries have 82 percent.

At the sixth Arab summit meeting in Algiers, the Arab oil-producing countries decided to take "special measures with a view to upholding the oil supply of the African brother countries." A topic now being discussed under the aegis of the Economic Commission for Africa and the Organization for African Unity is the feasibility of letting "the African producer countries take all those measures which are necessary to guarantee the African countries access to crude oil for all time." In conjunction with the avowed pledge, "Venezuela's oil is Latin America's oil," the idea of a common oil market has been born within ARPEL, the joint organization of state-owned oil companies in South America. In ASCOPE, an oil council recently set up by the countries of Southeast Asia, a share-out plan for oil is proposed which would obligate the oil-producing member countries "to give the nonproducing members preferential access to crude oil."

Summing up, we can make this observation about the future oil market: uncertainty is great not only about how much oil there is on the market but also about how the giant firms and the large oil-importing, industrialized countries will act precisely because the future oil supply is so precarious.

For several reasons national governments will play an ever bigger role and accordingly energy supply will be more and more imbued with considerations of foreign policy. Capital requirements are so great, planning periods are so long and constraints are so rigid that energy systems can scarcely be managed by private firms alone.

To complicate the picture, the oil-importing industrialized countries may be forced to pursue knotty negotiations toward the 1990s on how to allocate the then steadily diminishing oil produced among the different countries.

One possible way to reduce the increase in oil consumption is to steer toward a less oil-intensive economy. Obviously, some of that will be done automatically by way of higher oil prices. Another possible and supplementary way is to invest in a forceful oil-savings program.

But in that case who is going to save? Should everyone cut down by an equal amount, or should the countries that now use the most save the most? Should European and American cars be made to consume half as much gasoline in 1990 as they do today, or should the American cars be made to consume just as much in 1990 as the European cars do now? What social conflicts will be touched off, in the United States and Southern Europe for instance, by an energy policy which calls for a lower rate of increase in GNP? Conversely, what foreign policy will be required, say of the United States, to provide just enough energy for the American economy so as to avoid internal conflicts? And to what external conflicts will that foreign policy lead?

Presumably the energy commodities of oil, uranium, coal, and natural gas will be sucked into the global power struggle between North and South, between East and West. Perhaps the most ascerbic conflicts will arise among the oil-importing members of the industrialized world, chiefly the United States, the European community, and Japan.

For all these reasons it is nearly impossible to say when the transition will occur. The date (which strictly speaking is a time period) will depend on a long string of factors, some of which are controllable by the individual states.

Now what does the picture look like for Sweden? At present Sweden accounts for about 1.1 percent of the world's oil consumption; that oil represents about 70 percent of our energy use. Will that pattern stay the same even after world oil production has stagnated? Indeed, do we stand chances of carving out a larger share, or will we perhaps bring up the rear and have to make do with a smaller share? This is something we cannot possibly know, of course, and yet the queston of how much oil and uranium might be put at our disposal during the 1990s is critical for Sweden's future energy policy.

Here are some other factors that bear upon future developments in the energy sphere:

Our demand for energy depends on how our economy looks, which in its turn will depend on trends in the world economy *and* on what role we choose to play therein. For instance, is the Swedish industrial output contemplated in a recent official energy forecast for the 1990s internationally plausible in the first place? Here a number of options are in hand, and the choices presumably have great importance for how much energy we need.

Under what terms and conditions can we import energy technologies and commodities? It is not unreasonable to assume that countries and/or big firms want to take advantage of our dependence on them in the energy sphere and not only charge high prices but also wrest other concessions from us in regard to foreign and trade policies. Such concessions may be sought both for exports of Swedish uranium and imports of oil or coal. It is common knowledge that the United States, the Soviet Union, and China command the world's really big coal deposits. And countries close by such as Poland are also amply endowed with coal.

What environmental consequences are we prepared to accept? The acidification of land and water is no doubt the best example: much of the adverse effect comes from sulfur which is emitted in Western Europe. Just how seriously we rate this acidification will manifestly affect both our foreign policy and our domestic energy policy.

What new energy technologies are to be taken from abroad? New energy technologies, mainly for coal and uranium use, demand heavy inputs of research and development, for which we cannot reckon on being wholly independent. Hence we are partly reduced to buying systems from the outside and adapting them to Swedish conditions. Renewable energy sources are partly easier to exploit, and here we can achieve some degree of independence.

This general discussion should suffice to demonstrate that our transition from an oil-dominated economy is amenable to our own actions but that we can be subjected to external pressures. Seen from the point of view of future study, this sphere seems to be one of the more central and, at the same time, least discussed issues.

The Terms of Transition

Breeder technology is a logical and long-awaited sequel to present-day nuclear-power engineering. Similarly, the fuels synthesized from coal, heavy oils, and other materials, evolve naturally from today's coal and petrochemical industries.

Switching energy supply bases is not the outcome of a single big decision but rather the sum total of a great many small ones. And if now we want to steer this transition in one or the other direction, it follows that the decision-making process will be complicated.

In broad outline, it looks as though we have two conceivable lines of development for long-term energy supplies:

The one is a logical sequel to today's and tomorrow's (1980s) energy supply and can be called a *coal and/or breeder solution.* There coal (together with various heavy oils and tar sands, and similar materials) plays the role of raw material for synthetic fuels in liquid or gaseous form, whereas the breeder primarily delivers electricity. Limited amounts of renewable energy sources, such as solar panels, can also be imagined. Here we have elected to assign coal and breeders to the same category.

Both of them fit well into today's energy supply systems (and therefore may become tomorrow's). The components grow naturally and gradually into one another.

The second solution is based in all essentials on *renewable sources* and represents a radical departure from today's situation and trends. The base may be sun for heating; hydropower, wind, and perhaps solar cells for electric power generation; biomass for fuel production; and so on. Limited amounts of stored energy sources might be envisioned for fuel production.

Although both lines of development have sufficient potential for coping with the energy supply, there are great differences between them. By a rough count, the whole world is now earmarking twenty times more research and development resources for the coal and/or breeder solution than for the renewable solution.

To be sure, one can think of combinations among renewable energy sources, coal, and breeder reactors. Nonetheless we have elected to abstract the alternatives, mainly because there are so many imponderables in the "natural" solution (i.e., coal and/or breeders) that it is justified to hold a door open for a solution which contains neither fossil fuels nor nuclear power. Yet another reason is our hypothesis that the two solutions impose such varying demands on organizational structure, for instance, that they cannot be combined as a matter of course.

The most important differences and imponderables associated with various solutions are the following:

The *environmental effects*, which, as noted earlier, differ considerably. We are pretty familiar with the environmental and safety problems posed by breeders and coal, even though we do not know so much about how to remedy them and about how much that would cost. The renewable energy sources seem to pose much smaller environmental problems.

In terms of *social organization*, the two solutions presumably differ. The coal and/or breeder solution comes with highly capital-intensive technology that is used in large plants. From this there also follows the need for strongly centralized organization. The renewable solution is more geographically dispersed and as such might be more decentralized organizationally and economically. Some production of equipment can be very capital-intensive. The two solutions are probably dissimilar in their division of responsibilities among local, regional, and central bodies as well as between private and public bodies. But we shall return to this matter.

In terms of *foreign policy*, the solutions differ again. As far as Sweden is concerned we must import technology no matter what strategy we choose, especially if we put our reliance on capital-intensive plants. In the case of coal, moreover, we must import raw materials and/or finished fuels. In the case of breeders we have to be fitted into an international nuclear power system. As for the renewable sources, we still do not know what particular sort of foreign dependence these may involve.

Economic aspects. It is very difficult at this time to know what energy prices may be involved in either of the strategies. Coal technologies for synthetic fuels and the breeder programs have both been subjected to steep cost rises, and the forecasts of future energy prices are being revised upwards in stages. A different picture emerges on the renewable side. At present, electricity from sources such as photovoltaic cells is much more expensive than the going price of electricity, but the costs are on their way down. (In 1969 such cells cost Skr 2,000 per peak-watt, by 1976 they were down to Skr 75. The price will have to go down to between Skr 1 and 2 to be competitive today.) The big question is if and when the costs of electricity from solar engineering will fall below the increasing costs of electricity from coal or breeder reactors. This observation also holds for the other energy technologies. To round out the picture, the solutions differ in the quality of energy they provide. It is possible that space heating in the future will be relatively cheap if solar panels are mass-produced, while the price of electricity will be relatively high. The price of fuel may also be high depending on the method used to produce it.

Hence the uncertainties surrounding both strategies are great and of varying character. It follows that there are compelling reasons to preserve freedom of action; in any event, no once-and-for-all decision should be made at this time. We simply do not know enough about each strategy to permit outright rejection or acceptance.

A central question is whether the problem is of current urgency as the 1970s draw to a close. For instance, no one expects breeder reactors to play any major role for the supply of electric power until the years 1995–2000. But that is no reason for waiting. The next ten to fifteen years will decide how much freedom of action we have vis-à-vis the breeder reactors.

This can be illustrated with present-day nuclear power, which in Sweden is not likely to play a more palpable role in energy supply until the beginning of the 1980s. At the same time a parliamentary majority deemed it impossible in 1975 to rule out nuclear power altogether. But when did the policy makers really tie themselves down? Was it in 1970, 1965, 1960, or 1955?

The question admits of no easy answer, of course, but it seems as though a series of decisions was taken during 1955–1965 which in practice made nuclear power necessary in 1975. Noticeable among these decisions which chiefly bore down on the consumer side, in particular the reduction of electricity tariffs in 1963 and the active promotion of electrically heated homes. Further, alternatives to nuclear-based electrical power were pushed aside, above all the provision of back pressure by the local authorities.

But the reactors comprise only some of the components in the nuclear power program. The individual generating units must be served by a vast infrastructure consisting of mines, enrichment plants, reprocessing plants perhaps, waste storage, large (800 kV) electric networks, standby power adapted to the characteristics of nuclear power, a full-fledged organization to run the system, and so on. So far we have only begun to build the first components in a nuclear power system.

The foregoing example—which will be developed later in chapter 7—illustrates that a new (energy) technology is not introduced with a single decision but through a series of subdecisions, drawn out in this case over perhaps a twenty-year period.

We shall come back to these problems in the following chapters. What is quite clear, however, is that it takes a long time to change the energy system and that therefore we must *now* prepare the system we want to see in Sweden in ten to thirty years. And since, as we noted earlier, it is still too early to choose, we consider it important to put our chips on freedom of action.

Later on we shall discuss these questions in greater detail. Here we simply shall identify some points that we think make a long time perspective imperative:

Research and development take a long time, especially for large and complex systems. It is not unusual for ten years to elapse from idea to prototype, with ten more years or so to go from prototype to full-scale use. In view of these long research and development periods, commitments are sometimes made to systems about which information is poor—after all, that knowledge does not come until after the results of research and development projects are in hand. Because of these long periods, moreover, it is hard to switch to another system without incurring substantial delays.

The design of the consumer side bears crucially on the cost of switching from one energy source to another. If residential heating is based on direct electric-resistance heating, it will be very expensive to switch over in a later stage to, say, solar heat plus heat pumps. In contrast, a water-based heating system is more flexible and can be more easily connected to district, electric and solar heating facilities. At the same time it is more expensive to install. The more houses that are exclusively designed for direct electric-resistance heating, the more expensive it will be to cut loose from nuclear power, for example.

The constraints of big systems. Nuclear power and its nuclear fuel cycle are one example of an energy technology where there are a great many components with long lead times and high capital intensity. This, in combination with the vast uncertainties about future costs, which are known from experience to characterize complicated technologies, means that the systems are not only built up gradually but also gradually contain more and more sunken costs. As a consequence of the step-by-step decision-making process, a system may evolve which, seen overall, has substantially higher costs than the alternatives even though it did not look that way at each step. The longer the road traveled toward one system, the cheaper the alternatives must be to permit switching to another road.

Organizational inertia and dynamic conservatism. Superimposed upon the economic constraints are other constraints that are mostly social in nature. Every technology requires an organization, a pattern of cooperation among individuals who together form a social pattern. Other technologies impose other demands, and to introduce a new technology is to imply that the social pattern must be changed. Here lies a cardinal component of inertia: the "sunken costs" of individuals with their present working routines and present competence. This "human capital" resists change.

The interorganizational division of responsibilities. Our studies on the evolution of Swedish energy policy have established that the division of responsibilities among organized groups—the electricity producers, electricity distributors, consumers, and so forth—plays a big role in the technical and organizational design. To some extent the responsibility for this system of rules is borne by the legislative and executive branches of government, and it also turns out that such things as new energy technologies make it necessary to change the rules more often than not. That was the case when hydropower was introduced, and the same holds for nuclear power. The renewable energy sources will be no exception. Here there is considerable inertia—not to mention resistance—in the face of some new technologies, at the same time as other new technologies slip through much more easily.

Summing up, we think the industrialized world is on the road that leads to a coal and/or breeder solution in the second time perspective. For a reader examining the different points we have made will find that all of them favor this solution in preference to the renewable-sources alternative. The road goes by way of the increased use of coal in the first time perspective and a build-up of the whole nuclear fuel cycle for light-water reactors.

So it seems as if freedom of action in choosing the next generation of energy sources will not come of its own accord. It will require active efforts mounted by Parliament and Cabinet. One important reason for this is that several of the uncertainties felt about the next generation's energy sources do not relate to technical-economic factors but to their impact on the process of social change. This is a state of affairs for which the energy sector cannot, nor should it, assume sole responsibility.

Given the current division of responsibilities between government authorities and the energy supply sector, it would be more appropriate to say that the door to the coal and/or breeder solution is being opened bit by bit, while the door to the renewable-sources alternative is being closed bit by bit.

In practice, therefore, a policy which seeks to create freedom of action requires a series of measures that open both doors gradually. Society in general and the energy sector in particular must not allow either solution to become more expensive to implement while the other becomes cheaper and cheaper if freedom of action is to be maintained. So the task is to find a least common denominator. At the same time, it is quite clear that such a balanced policy will itself draw upon resources and lead to various conflicts.

A policy for freedom of action must be guarded against ambush. But how should such a policy be formulated? What issues should be its targets? Where must measures be taken? What division of responsibilities is necessary? We shall address these questions in subsequent chapters.

4
Limits to Freedom of Action

Introduction

IN THIS CHAPTER we try to clarify some important points to consider in order to give us freedom of action in the choice of future energy supply systems. These principal points will be developed in the following three chapters, after which the discussion will be summarized in the final chapter.

Freedom of action is not an absolute that can be quantified. Nevertheless we evidently have more or less of it in any particular decision-making situation. Such freedom can be increased or decreased. Over the very long term (many hundreds of years), of course, freedom of action (latitude or room for maneuvering) is very great. That is because over such a great period we can imagine a brand-new infrastructure, the breakthrough of a new cultural pattern. In the short and medium terms (ten of years) freedom of action is limited by the existing infrastructure: roads, buildings, educational systems, cultural patterns, and so forth. Just how limiting these factors are in any one decision-making situation, say, for the society's choice of energy sources, is something we can influence by adopting various measures that affect the total energy system. Up to the time a decision is made, for instance, *different* courses of action can be studied through analysis of lockstep or jamming mechanisms and deliberate avoidance of such rigidities, through research and development projects that concentrate on competing or supplementary alternatives, and more. The degree to which we can affect freedom of action will depend, of course, on how much time we have, on what measures already have been taken, and on how concerned we are.

To "plan for freedom of action" is to employ a phrase that is very much in vogue: they are the current "buzzwords." The reality is usually more dismal. In practice, freedom of action is nothing one possesses or preserves; it is created by committing resources of different kinds: intellectual resources, by which efforts are made to understand what the problem looks like; economic resources, by which investments whose outcomes are uncertain are made; emotional and political resources to hold at bay all the more or less powerful interest groups whose minds are already made up. Creating freedom of action may also imply that conflicts among different interest groups will become more explicit. Hence there are fairly natural explanations why there are so few good examples of implemented planning for increased freedom of action.

Chapter 3 ended with a hypothesis stating that the energy supply system is on its way toward a coal and/or breeder strategy as a long-term solution. If freedom of action is to be created, then this solution requires no further attention. Freedom of action is needed for the second main alternative, the renewable energy sources.

We used the simile of two doors. At present neither door stands wide open, though both stand ajar; today, we enjoy some freedom of action for both alternatives. Powerful forces are stirring themselves to open the one door—the one that leads towards the coal and/or breeder society. Much smaller resources are being staked on opening the other door—the one that leads towards the renewable-sources society.

At the same time a number of measures have been taken elsewhere in society—outside the energy supply sector—which tend bit by bit to close one door and open the other. Such measures are intended to regulate the size and thrust of private and public consumption, the physical design of dwelling units and urban settlements, and so forth.

Superimposed on such essentially technical and economic mechanisms, which try to prize open the one door and nail shut the other, is yet another force. Every technical system presupposes some form of organization, consisting of people with varying levels of education and professional competence, roles, expectations, and hopes about their own and the organization's future. This group of people constitute an inertia factor. They offer resistance to change and most readily accept those technical solutions which signify small changes in social organization.

In various respects a policy meant, say, to give Parliament and Cabinet greater freedom to choose future technology for energy supply will be construed as a threat by those groups who advocate one solution or the other. So the question, freedom of action *for whom?* follows right on the heels of the question, *for what?*

We have chosen the following three angles of approach:

How much energy do we really need? In other words, how do we accommodate our own living standard and our need for energy? And how does this energy requirement develop over time (chapter 4: "How much energy do we really need?" and chapter 5)?

What types of energy do we need? The next generation of energy sources will deliver different types of energy. A coal and/or breeder solution first of all provides liquid or gaseous fuels and electricity. A renewable-sources solution partly provides other types of energy. Our need for energy must therefore be discussed in these terms as well (chapter 4:"What types of energy do we need?" and chapter 6).

Can we control the energy supply system? And if so, where can the control be deployed (chapter 4: "Can we control the energy supply system?" and chapter 7).

How Much Energy Do We Really Need?

Generally speaking, it is obvious that the increasing rate of energy consumption bears crucially upon freedom of action in the choice among future energy supply systems.

The rate at which we must introduce new sources will very much depend on how rapidly the demand for energy grows. The higher the rate of increase, the earlier that new increments must be introduced and the faster their contributions will have to grow.

Although many factors determine the speed with which a new energy source can be introduced, we wish to point out the organizational factor in particular. It takes time to build up a body of knowledge, a competent organization, and so forth. Hence new energy sources demand a head start which, from this viewpoint, deviates as little as possible from the existing sources.

By way of example, we can take the discussion of nuclear power and wind power. For the former there exists a decision-making process with licensing rules, a production organization complete with subcontractors, which without too much trouble can build one more reactor or generating unit with an output of 5 TWh. Corresponding amounts of electricity from wind power might require 2,500 units, each capable of generating 2,000 MWh (1 MW output per unit), making it necessary to arrange sites, obtain permission, secure the approval of regulatory agencies, and so forth. It takes time to build up an organization and a decision-making process capable of providing perhaps 5 TWh per annum with wind power.

The same rationale can be applied to energy saving. Saving 5 TWh of electricity, say through housing insulation, requires adaptation by the capital market, the training of personnel, and increased production capacity in the building materials industry, and this also takes time.

It follows that cutting down on the rate of increase in energy usage is an essential measure for increasing freedom of action.

We can speak of two groups of measures to reduce the energy usage.

The first group seeks to render energy usage more effective with different types of thrift measures, such as additional insulation in houses, cars that skimp on gasoline, new methods for manufacturing paper pulp, and the like. Such measures are sometimes called "technical fixes."

These measures are affected by the movement of energy prices. These prices depend in part on decisions taken by government (taxes, for instance) and in part on uncertain political and geological conditions. The will to invest in such measures is also affected by what consumers assume about the future movement of energy prices.

The second group signifies that consumption patterns and to a certain degree life styles are affected. By way of example we can take an increased investment in public services at the expense of private consumption, increased investment in public transportation, and, related to that perhaps, a changed system of urban and regional planning. It can be said that such measures do not cost money primarily; they entail changing values in order to influence consumption patterns.

One example of a potentially important value change is to put greater emphasis on work and employment not only as a production factor but also as a value in its own right. For the one who works, this could mean both a lowering of labor productivity—measured in traditional terms—and changes in the consumption pattern such that other consequences for the economy can be imagined. The attitude toward work and its role has shifted during the twentieth century and there is reason to believe that this will continue. Here it should be borne in mind, of course, that it is impossible and meaningless to define any costs for measures of this kind.

It takes different amounts of time for changes in energy usage to be felt. Adjustments to higher energy prices are made much faster than changes in people's values.

Hence the importance of "technical fix" measures is to buy time. But if nothing else is done energy usage, because of the way the economy is shaped, will increase as soon as certain physical limits have been reached. The impact on consumption affords further opportunities and taken together with the technical fix measures can exert more downward pressure on the rate of increase in energy usage. But is is doubtful whether such measures can achieve zero growth in energy usage over the long term.

Another dimension can be added to the foregoing by saying that the level of long-term energy usage is not decisive. If energy can be tapped without negative consequences in the form of environmental despoliation, political bindings, or inordinate economic inputs, there is no reason to hold back the rate of increase in usage. That point is worth bearing in mind. For the moment we do not know whether energy can be tapped in that way, but it seems clear to us that an alternative based solely on solar energy is feasible in the long run.

What Types of Energy Do We need?

So far we have been discussing energy usage and its rate of increase as if all kinds of energy could be tarred with the same brush. In so doing we have also assumed that 1 MWh in the form of oil is just as useful as 1 MWh in the form of electricity.

A lengthy discussion of the plausibility of this assumption has been waged. The conclusion is that there is so simple answer but that different types of energy usage must be distinguished. Underlying the discussion are two thoughts.

The first is that different energy forms vary in quality. Quality is an index of usefulness and diversity. Electricity can be used for electronic processes, mechanical work, transportation, and heating. Oil can be used for mechanical work, transportation, and heating, but with greater losses at the point of usage. Oil does not lend itself at all to electronic processes unless it is first converted into electricity—with heavy losses. By and large hot water has no application other than space heating.

The second thought is that different applications vary in their need for quality. To illustrate, rooms can be heated with electricity, an oil furnace, and hot water coming from a district heating plant, while electrolytic processes require electricity.

It follows that types of energy usage can be studied not only with reference to what energy forms they *actually use* but also according to which energy forms—and which energy quality— will be *sufficient*.

We shall develop this reasoning further in chapter 6. Let us make do for the moment by stating that today's energy supply is primarily based on oil and electricity, both of which are of high quality. This implies that we use energy of high quality even where we could get by with energy of lower quality.

An analysis of Swedish energy usage in quality terms shows that about 42 percent is low-temperature heat (space heating) and that the dominant uses for energy of high quality are process heat (25 percent) and transportation (19 percent).

Should energy of high quality become scarce, therefore, the social fabric would have to become one which saves on materials and transportation. That would affect not only urban and regional planning and the pattern of building coverage, but also product design and the economy's thrust.

Services such as nursing and child care draw less energy per krona and per employee than the production of goods does. So a society that puts greater emphasis on such services saves more energy than a society which puts greater emphasis on goods consumption. But the production of services is also less demanding of high-quality energy than the goods production sector. We may therefore assume that a services-oriented society uses relatively less energy of high quality than a goods-producing society with today's mix of production and consumption. At some future time, of course, one can imagine other patterns of goods consumption (bicycle vacations instead of chartered flights, books instead of powerboat cruises) which are less energy-intensive and thus help to cut down on the energy intensity of private consumption.

Seen from the quality viewpoint, the coal and/or breeder solution makes a logical sequel to the present-day energy supply. It yields energy forms of high quality.

The renewable solution does not necessarily have the same characteristics. Although the solar energy that falls on the earth (insolation) is admittedly of high quality, it is only the energy forms that we get with collection techniques that are essential. Solar collectors, the devices that convert radiant heat from the sun into hot water, are relatively cheap. At present it costs much more to produce the same amount of energy via, say, electricity from photocells. But as we discussed earlier the cost picture is very unclear.

The next generation of energy sources can thus be converted with varying ease into energy carriers of different energy quality. This point, we think, has great importance when it comes to finding measures which hold the door open to the renewable solution.

Can We Control the Energy Supply System?

To what extent does the organizational design of the energy supply system limit governmental freedom of action?

There seem to be characteristics which make it hard for an outsider to steer the choice among energy technologies. In other words, there exists an innate inertia which must be understood and counteracted.

There are compelling reasons to believe that a policy which confers greater freedom of action in the choice of future energy technology on Parliament and Cabinet, and with that on the political process, will not be favorably perceived by all parties concerned. On the contrary, such a policy might generate sharp conflicts.

Suppose we have to choose between two alternatives for a technical system. Those who advocate alternative one want us to opt for this course as soon as possible, and the same goes for the advocates of alternative two. Any postponement of a decision (whether in favor of one alternative or the other) will be construed by both parties as a threat. The pressure to decide as early as possible is extremely strong.

One example of how such a decision-making process has operated in the real world is the project to build the Swedish fighter aircraft *Viggen*. One of the lessons taught by this project is that every big system contains a "dynamic force" in the form of investments in capital and equipment, organizational structures, ideas put forth, personal careers, and, last but not least, in mental images of what the problem to be solved actually looks like. Is this a high-technology war or a guerilla war?

It is important that decision makers be certain that these producer interests are not to be found inside any one organization or business enterprise. Quite the contrary, for virtually every major technical project it is a coalition of private interests, a combination of suppliers, subcontractors, and government agencies which more often than not act as clients and/or regulators.

Obviously this type of dynamic force, of producer interests, will also be found within the energy sphere. Thus the introduction of hydropower was influenced by powerful interests asserted both by buyers (the electricity supply system) and by those who supplied buyers (electrical equipment), the construction industry, and so forth. Similarly, when demand for electricity expanded during the 1920s and 1930s, there was close cooperation between electricity producers and distributors on the one hand and the electrical appliances industry on the other.

Powerful interests are thus at work striving to secure early adoption of the one solution or the other. The rational motive for this purpose is that substantial resources can sometimes be saved by concentrating early on a specific system.

But often there are other and deeper-lying motives. Several organizational sociologists have pointed out that firms (and other organizations, too) are impelled by a nearly fundamental instinct to reduce uncertainty and accordingly act to make their situation as predictable as possible. A policy where government wants to preserve its freedom of action will be perceived by large and powerful groups as adding to their uncertainty as compared with a policy where government throws its weight behind a single technology.

Having said this, we have also said that a policy for increased freedom of action is not only a matter of choosing a technology but also a matter of how to strike these choices. What do the organizations look like? What is the division of responsibilities between, say, the State Power Board, municipal distributors of electricity, homeowners, the National Board of Urban Planning, the National Housing Board, Parliament, and Cabinet?

Rigid commitments to any one type of technology emanate from two quarters: not only from the producers of the utility in question but also from the users. The technical systems on the producer and consumer sides become enmeshed in one another, which is just what happens when you fasten a zipper.

Vital parts of this "interlocking" process start to move even before the technology is there. For instance, electrically heated homes were initially promoted because cheap nuclear power was thought to be imminent, and so the merchandising got under way before any big nuclear power plants were operating.

Hence a new technology enters the picture in response to the operation of "push" and "pull" forces: push from the producer, pull from the consumer. The patterns of expectation of individuals and organizations seem to matter a great deal for the direction that these forces take.

Expressed somewhat more systematically, we have here four roles which are important, namely the energy producer, the energy consumer, the appliance producer, and central government (Parliament and Cabinet). A new technology will be introduced on the energy production side as an interplay among the first three of these. It will then be up to central government to lay down the ground rules for the performance of this four-part drama. We shall discuss these questions at greater length in chapter 7.

5
Energy Policy: On Goal Conflicts in Society

Introduction

THERE ARE OBVIOUS connections between the way society is organized and the amount of energy of different kinds that is needed. The present chapter will be devoted to a more detailed review of these problems. Our material is partly based on sub-studies that were carried out in connection with the future study.

Our interest is focused chiefly on those connections between energy-system design and social organization which surface during political debate. This is where goal conflicts are treated and priorities are decided. Since 1973 and 1973, moreover, the debate on energy policy has concentrated on means to weigh the advantages of an abundance of energy against the drawbacks which the necessary energy supply system brings in its train.

So far during most of the twentieth century a rising level of prosperity has been held to necessitate a constantly increasing energy supply. Although this thesis has been stated most explicitly in the postwar period, the modes of thinking were fully developed long before then. Already at the inception of the Swedish State Power Board, glowing word pictures were painted of the increased prosperity that the expansion of hydropower would bring, not least for the far northern inland area (Norrland). By and large this basic ethos has carried over into the 1970s. Expansion of the energy supply has been subordinated to and steered by the insistence on rapid economic growth.

But bit by bit the design of energy supply has come into conflict with other social goals. The blockade during World War II illustrated the perils of our dependence on imported fuels. When oil imports shot up after the war a number of warning voices were raised in the early 1950s, and the Swedish commitment to nuclear power was motivated in part by the desire to hold back these imports. The design of the energy system thus helped to put the demand for a larger energy supply into growing conflict with the demand for international independence.

Other conflicts began to brew during the 1950s. The expansion of hydropower wrought lasting changes in lakes and rivers and gradually intensified the opposition. This meant that the energy system component of economic policy gradually came into conflict with a policy for conserving the environment. Conflicts of this type have been waxing. The energy sector now visits its environmental impacts on more and more fields of activity, as witnessed by the acidification of air and water and emissions of carcinogenic substances from fossil fuels.

The choice of energy technology also affects our dependence on other countries—in one way when we import commodities like oil and coal, in another way when we form an integral part of an international system such as the nuclear power fuel cycle. Not only that, but the choice of energy technology also has organizational and institutional consequences.

The main inference we draw from the choice of energy supply system is this: above all it will put the wish for sustained economic growth more or less on a collision course with other wishes, such as for a clean environment, codetermination, and national independence.

This can be illustrated with oil. On the one hand, it is a prerequisite for production and hence for the economy. On the other hand, it contributes to the acidification of our lakes, spreads carcinogenic substances, sucks us into a dependence on imports, and so forth. So a discussion of future oil usage really boils down to a discussion of how important these different contributions are relative to each other.

To substitute nuclear-based electricity for oil signifies that the environmental disturbances will change character as will the dependence on foreign countries, added to which are new problems associated with radioactive waste management. To replace electricity from nuclear power with hydropower will trigger conflicts between the desire for an abundance of electricity and ecological interests.

Every type of energy comes with its own set of conflicts. Nor does energy policy deal with energy in general but with specific types of energy. The important thing is not the number of TWh that are used but how these TWh are produced—via oil combustion, nuclear power, or hydropower. In other words, there is no reason to have zero growth for energy usage if this is based, say, on renewable energy sources. The goal set by the 1975 parliamentary decision on energy policy in Sweden, which was to cut down on the rate of increase in energy usage from 4.5 percent to 2 percent, should therefore not be interpreted as setting energy saving as a goal unto itself. Rather, it should be viewed as a draft of the desire to hold back oil combustion, the expansion of nuclear power, and hydropower.

We now take up the connections between energy usage and different social goals. The consequences of these goals will not be weighed together here; our main object is to introduce the links. That is, this chapter sheds some light on the room for maneuvering available to energy policy makers in relation to specified social goals.

Energy and Economics

Energy supply has long been subordinated to the insistence on increasing production, which in its turn has been necessary to abolish mass poverty. Lately, economic growth per se has been regarded almost as something sacrosanct and as a necessary antecedent to full employment. Gradually, however, economic policy has taken on more and more dimensions, and it is now necessary to discuss some goal conflicts. On the one hand, there is the goal of holding back the rate of increase in energy usage; on the other, a number of goals for economic policy: full employment, a high increase in real income, and a more even income distribution.

Our reasoning does not imply taking any stand for or against economic growth but only an attempt to sort out the connections between economic growth and energy usage. We assume that the energy supply will not pose problems for other fields, that is, we assume that the price of energy will reflect the whole cost society incurs to provide and utilize energy.

The problems we encounter are bound up with the time perspective. It seems reasonable to talk about three time horizons, each with its own array of problems and possibilities.

The short-term perspective, when factories, machines, buildings, and dwellings lie where they currently lie, the equipment is given and so are the administrative routines. Rapid changes in energy supply and/or energy prices can then threaten both employment and welfare. The time horizon is on the order of zero to as much as five years.

The medium-long time perspective, when the array of machines, buildings, factories, and dwellings can be influenced and along with that the amount of energy that is expended to solve any given problem, measures can be taken which affect the relative size of manufacturing industry, the transportation sector, the health/medical sector, and others. With that, too, leverage is exerted on the increase in real incomes and the distribution of employment between, say, production for private and public consumption. This time perspective also contains possibilities for partial substitution of electricity for fuel and vice versa, as well as possibilities for more effective energy usage. Here we concern ourselves with the horizon adopted by the Employment Commission and the Finance Ministry's Economic Planning Council with its long-term (five to fifteen years) surveys.

The very long time perspective, where one is not tied down so much by today's real capital in the form of machinery, equipment, and so forth: here the limits to freedom of action lie more in what institutions we have built up—what mechanisms we have to guarantee welfare and its distribution, the extent to which a person's income is coupled to or disengaged from his or her participation in the labor market, and so on. Here the macroeconomic angle of approach must be widened by ideas which derive chiefly from social psychology and social anthropology. The time perspective encompasses fifteen to twenty years or longer.

Some reports recently published by the Secretariat for Future Studies are primarily concerned with the medium-long time perspective, which roughly embraces the time within which we must begin to supplement oil and nuclear power (light-water reactors). Seen from the energy supply vantage, the very long time perspective coextends with the period within which coal

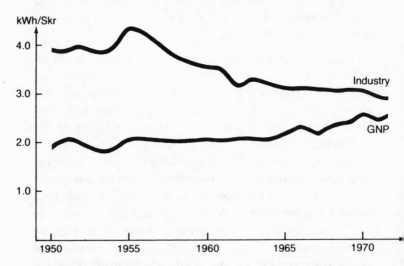

Fig. 6. Energy intensity in Sweden's GNP and industrial output in 1950–1972, kWh per krona of value added measured in 1965 prices.

and/or breeders and renewable energy sources will have to begin playing an important role.

These studies show that Sweden's economy has become increasingly energy-intensive over the years. Energy consumption has outstripped the growth of GNP.

A breakdown by economic sectors, such as industry, agriculture, transportation, and commerce, shows that industry is an exception; as a whole industry has been using energy more and more efficiently (as seen in table 3).

TABLE 3

PRODUCTIVITY DEVELOPMENT (OUTPUT PER UNIT OF INPUT)
IN SWEDISH INDUSTRY.
Index: 1955 = 100.

Year	Production (expressed as value added)	Capital stock	Labor	Energy
1955	100	100	100	100
1960	129	126	101	116
1965	184	165	104	143
1970	233	203	96	174

The development of energy and labor per unit of output (expressed as value added by manufacture) is set out in figure 7 (which is based on table 3).

Industry has obtained thus more output for each unit of energy used. All other sectors (agriculture, transportation, commerce) have experienced declining output per unit of energy. The connections between energy usage and labor productivity is another question that has been discussed. To what extent do productivity increments depend on using up more energy?

That question is hard to answer. Generally speaking, a higher degree of productivity is attained by putting more machinery and other equipment at people's disposal (i.e., the capital intensity increases). Machines use energy. But new machines, to which the old are giving way, usually use less energy per unit of output. The question to ask is how strong each of these trends is: the introduction of machines that require more and more energy, while producing more output, and the trend for newer machines to use energy with increasing efficiency. In short, great importance attaches to the pace of technological advance.

In *industry* increasing labor productivity has not necessarily increased energy usage per unit of output. In other words, advancing technology has prevailed over the introduction of more machines. Today, man as an energy source is of virtually no importance in industry—nor does a higher degree of mechanization to improve the working environment matter from the energy standpoint. Conversely, the importance of process monitoring and control has increased. There is, of course, a conceivable connection here between the energy used in various processes, how well they are controlled, and how much work effort is required.

In the *transport sector* labor productivity has increased as energy usage per unit of output has increased. Here, presumably, the increased capital intensity has served to shorten transport times, that is, speed has increased. Trains are replaced by trucks, buses by automobiles, and so forth. In so doing one buys time with energy.

In the *forestry and farming sector* labor productivity has also been raised with a sharply increased energy input, in the form of more tractors, more dryers, more artificial fertilizers. Energy from human muscle and animals (horses) has given way to machines, just as the yield per employed person has increased.

The *service sector,* finally, is poorly served by statistics, but the data available indicate that here again the energy required per

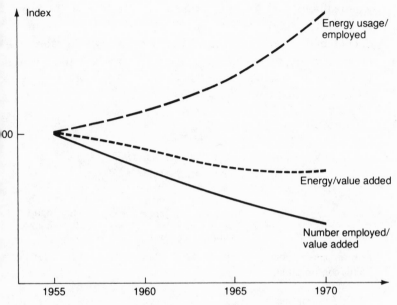

Fig. 7. Productivity development in Swedish industry.

unit of output has gone up with increasing labor productivity. One among several likely causes is the improved standard of physical facilities. We surround ourselves with more and more floor space in our offices and hospitals, for instance.

Now, one can say that comparisons of this sort are a bit misleading. There are other ways of replacing man by expending energy. For example, a labor-intensive but energy-saving material—such as leather—can be replaced by a labor-saving but energy-intensive material—such as plastic.

We have chosen another way to describe energy consumption so as to enhance our understanding of why it is on the rise. Instead of studying branches of industry, transportation, the housing sector, and so forth, we have studied energy usage for what the national income accounts usually call the "end use". This term refers to the amounts of energy and labor we devote to private consumption,[1] etc. For this purpose we have figured out how much energy and labor is required totally—both for direct production and for utilization (e.g., in space heating)—to cater to private consumption in its entirety. These figures have then been divided by the total consumption in Swedish kronor. Table 4 refers to conditions in 1970.

TABLE 4

DIRECT AND INDIRECT ENERGY USE IN DIFFERENT
SOCIAL SECTORS IN SWEDEN, 1970.

	Energy TWh	%	man-hours %	kWh/ Skr	man-hours/ Skr	kWh/ man-hour
Private consumption	191	44	36	3.1	0.026	119
Public consumption, central	19	4	8	1.7	0.044	39
Public consumption, local	23	5	15	1.2	0.051	24
Capital investment	58	13	20	2.2	0.017	47
Exports	135	31	19	4.7	0.011	115
Inventory changes	14	3	2			
Total use	434 TWh		6,130 million man-hours			

The purview of this table does not exceed the energy that is used in Sweden. For instance, private consumption includes a great many imported goods. The manufacture of these products draws energy abroad. On a rough count the energy content of imported merchandise can be estimated at 100 TWh. Since most of these imports go to private consumption we can say, as an approximation, that private consumption draws three-fourths of the energy we use in Sweden.

[1]Private consumption is thus understood to mean the purchases made by households of goods and services.

Seen functionally, the classification above is an arbitrary one. The public consumption accounted for by local authorities includes services which the households formerly performed, like day-care for children. Private consumption includes everything that we pay for by ourselves with our incomes, our rent allowances, and so forth.

A more detailed analysis gives the following picture for private and public (i.e., central government plus local authority) consumption (see tables 5 and 6). The figures given for private consumption pertain to 1969. The first table includes the energy content of imported goods, based on the assumption that this energy content is what it would have been had the goods been produced in Sweden.

TABLE 5

PATTERN OF PRIVATE CONSUMPTION IN SWEDEN, 1969
Expressed in energy per krona spent and hours worked
per krona spent

Average household consumption expressed in					
Skr	kWh	Private consumption	kWh/ Skr	man-hours/ Skr	kWh/ man-hour
5,678	10,700	Food	1.9	0.059	32
1,088	400	Beverages and tobacco	0.4	0.013	30
2,153	2,300	Clothing and shoes	1.1	0.051	21
1,056	1,100	Culture	1.0	0.045	23
426	900	Hygiene	2.0	0.031	66
1,656	4,600	Leisure	2.8	0.044	62
1,869	3,600	Furniture	1.9	0.044	43
2,106	2,300	Other goods and services	1.1	0.048	23
3,478	26,300	Private transport	7.6	0.042	180
3,194	2,700	Housing	0.8	0.010	82
922	19,400	Fuel and lighting	21.0	0.023	1,034
23,650	74,160	Average	3.1		

Note the small number of entries which dominate energy usage. Transportation, housing, food, and leisure account for about 85 percent of the energy used by households, but only 61 percent of the usage that private consumption maintains.

The tables show how the country's need for energy depends on how we as citizens elect to spend our money. On an average, every krona that is spent on private consumption draws nearly four times as much energy as a krona spent on, say, the operation of our health, medical, and social services.

How the energy requirement per man-hour has developed for different applications over the period 1960–1970 is shown in figure 8.

TABLE 6

PATTERN OF PUBLIC CONSUMPTION IN SWEDEN, 1968
Expressed in energy per krona and hours worked per krona.

Public consumption	kWh/Skr	man-hours/Skr	kWh/man-hour
Defense	1.52	0.030	51
Roads and streets	3.97	0.025	159
Education	0.74	0.030	25
Health services	0.88	0.050	18
Social services	0.87	0.059	15
Law enforcement	0.82	0.038	22
Other public administration	1.51	0.026	58

In 1970 private consumption demanded nearly five times more energy per hour worked than did the consumption of local-authority or municipal services. Perhaps the most striking aspect is that the intersectoral differences have increased so sharply. One reason for this is to be sought in the intensity of energy usage (kWh/Skr), which has increased more rapidly in goods production than in services production. The most important factor behind this development is the sharply increased labor productivity in the goods-producing sector. One of the reasons for this is that the share of consumer durables (automobiles, domestic appliances, and the like) in private consumption has been rising steadily. Typically, these goods require less and less labor for their manufacture and more and more energy when they are used. Not only that, but private consumption contains a broad array of imported articles—automobiles, for instance—which provide employment in the exporting country and above all draw energy in Sweden. Households also consume an ever greater part of their energy in direct form—to power appliances, run cars, heat homes, and so forth. So, in relative terms, the amount of energy required to produce consumer goods for households has fallen off, whereas the amount consumed to use these same goods is increasing. The future course of events will very much be swayed by whether or not this pattern is amenable to change.

Tables 5 and 6 and figure 8 can also illustrate certain weighing-up or trade-off problems. Sweden's totally available labor force can be deployed toward satisfying different components of the total living standard—housing, food, leisure, private automobile use, child care, old-age care, and so forth. In addition to labor every such area requires energy—but the *ratio* of manpower requirements to energy requirements varies sharply from one area to another. Transportation requires 180 kWh per man-hour while child care (not counting expenditures such as children's journeys to and from day nurseries) requires 15 kWh per man-hour. The difference has also increased over time.

It follows that the way in which we have chosen to shape our everyday lifestyles has influenced the way our energy usage has evolved.

We shall take these reflections as a starting point for a discussion of the connections between energy usage level, real income and employment in the longer run.

During the twentieth century we have had falling energy prices.

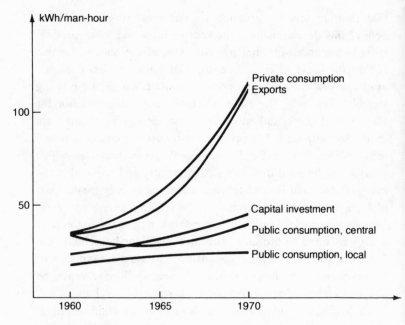

Fig. 8. Energy required per man-hour (average values) within different sectors in Sweden. Values obtained by dividing energy usage by number of hours worked within each sector (cf. table 4).

This trend was broken at the beginning of the 1970s, in all probability for good (see chapter 3). However, it is impossible to say how rapidly energy prices will rise or how stable the trend will be.

The trend itself will lower the rate of increase in energy usage. We are going to have fewer resources left over for other purposes, which means less scope for consumption. Not only that, but energy-thriftier technology will be gradually developed and become operational. Today, it is impossible to predict how fast this process may unfold and what impact technological development may have.

Rising energy prices also make energy conservation rewarding. One may ask how this will affect energy intensity in private and public consumption, in exports, and in other economic spheres.

Here certain guesses can be made. Space heating and the processing industry are believed of course to harbor the biggest
savings potentials. Space heating in particular absorbs much of
the energy required by the public sector (especially local government), whereas private consumption (housing aside) involves a
number of other energy-intensive components, too. It is reasonable therefore to assume that the differences of energy intensity
(kWh per krona, kWh per employed) which exist between public
and private consumption, for instance, will persist, and perhaps
increase, even after a vigorous conservation program is implemented.

If we want to arrest the accelerated rate of energy usage beyond
the level that is set by energy prices, additional measures will
have to be taken. Greater conservation will require additional
scope for capital investment and narrow the scope for consumption. Consumption will have to become less energy-intensive.

If higher standards of living are realized primarily by enlarging
the public sector (above all education and the many different
kinds of social services) rather than providing for more private
consumption, a less energy-intensive thrust for the economy will
result. This point is illuminated by the Economic Planning Council, which has also demonstrated that it will lower the rate of
expansion in industrial employment, for example.

The smaller the goods-producing sector is in relation to the
services sector, the lower the future increase in productivity will
be. After all, public services, such as nursing and education, are
essentially concerned with social relations, and there the human
being cannot be replaced by machines in the way that is feasible
in the goods-producing sector. So, turning the consumption pattern in this direction simultaneously denotes that increments of
productivity in the economy will taper off and that the upward
movement of real wages will be diminished.

It should be pointed out, however, that private consumption
contains not just energy-intensive segments such as housing and
transportation. Reading books, listening to stereo, collecting

stamps, and growing roses do not draw much energy. Obviously, we must not rule out the possibility that private consumption in the future may become less energy-intensive, but such a development is unlikely. Speaking negatively, if we do not want to accept a lowered rate of increase in real wages but still want to have an ambitious energy-conservation policy, somehow we must see to it that change in private consumption specifically zeroes in on energy-economizing activities. First we must discover how to go about limiting just those parts of private consumption that are energy-intensive (housing, automobiles, air travel, motorboats, the heating of cottages and other secondary dwellings, and so forth.)

Accordingly, we think there is a connection between the level of energy usage and the movement of real wages: we cannot restrain the former without restraining the latter. However, two factors attenuate this coupling, though we do not think they suffice to keep the two trends apart. The first is advancing technology. Obviously, it is next to impossible to predict what cost savings this development may bring. Estimates have been made, but the theoretical and data-processing difficulties are so great as to make the results highly uncertain. Another factor of possible importance is the absence of a macroeconomically accurate trade-off between investments in energy-saving measures and energy production. To the best of our knowledge, there is no study which either supports or refutes such an assertion. Even so, it can be noted that the scarcity of capital for manufacturing industry is so great as to assign a payoff period of five years to investments in energy saving, whereas the write-off period for, say, nuclear power is twenty-five years.

But, taking all things together, we think the previously mentioned conclusion will hold in the long run: restraining the rate of increase in energy usage will restrain the rise of wages. In other words, there is a conflict between the goal of restricting the rate of increase in energy usage and the goal of increasing private consumption.

This does not mean, however, that there are any long-term conflicts between the goal of holding down energy usage and the goal of upholding full employment. A policy which aims at zero growth in energy usage does not conflict with full employment. The energy-thrifty consumption pattern that is based on public services is also employment-intensive.

To say there is no connection between energy and employment for the country as a whole is not to suggest that such connections are absent at the local, regional, or industry-by-industry level. A vigorously pursued energy-conservation policy will probably accelerate the process of structural change in the business world. The geographic distribution of workplaces may be expected to change. The number of people employed in manufacturing may be expected to fall off more rapidly if we want to hold back the movement of real wages by backing the production of services. To maintain employment without resettling people to an inordinately great extent will presumably require relocation and labor-market policies with broader perspectives.

Combining the growth of real wages with a sharp reduction of increase in energy usage is going to be a tough job—unless we contemplate substantial changes in the mix of private consumption. But since the big energy-intensive items in that mix are the ordinary functions of life—food, travel, shelter, leisure—we think such changes are bound to take time.

An essential correlative question is this: just who consumes the energy-intensive items? Based on the sums that different households spend on food, clothing, leisure, and so forth (according to the 1969 Household Budget Survey) total household use of energy—direct and indirect—has been calculated. Figure 9 shows quite clearly that energy and income vary directly: the higher our income, the more energy we consume.

These figures, admittedly rough, show that, by and large, energy usage is proportional to income. Thus a household earning 50 percent higher real income after tax than another household consumes 50 percent more energy. The figures refer to average households, and today there is no evidence to permit discussing the differences between households for their consumption of energy when disposable income is at a certain level.

The energy tax may be the instrument to bring to bear on energy usage. Estimates show that levying higher taxes on electricity and heating oil hits the lower-income brackets relatively harder, while raising taxes on gasoline hits relatively harder at those with higher incomes.

The conflicts between energy policy and income distribution policy may be roughly summarized as follows. A straight-forward equalization of incomes does not appear to affect energy usage to any appreciable extent. Conversely different measures of energy policy, such as energy taxes, may have consequences for income distribution policy. Energy taxes can be offset in part by stepped-up transfer payments to avoid penalizing the worst-off more than the well-off. But the higher the compensation, the less the energy-conserving effect that can be attributed to energy taxes (even a compensation in toto, however, would still produce a certain energy-conserving effect).

One question we have not discussed in the present context is what consequences sharply increased energy taxes will have for our exporting industries. As yet we do not know whether we can have an energy pricing system which materially differs from that of our competitors on the international market.

Should we now wish to limit the rate of increase in energy usage, then whose consumption pattern is going to take the brunt? Is the present-day connection between energy usage and disposable income to be preserved? Or will those who now do not consume so much be given the opportunity to increase their use tomorrow at the expense of those who already consume vast amounts today?

In all likelihood an energy policy which aims at zero growth will make it necessary to push existing consumption in an energy-economizing direction. It would appear that more efficient energy,

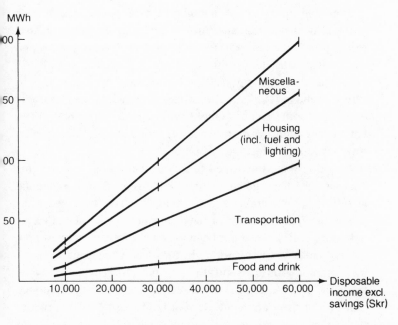

Fig. 9. Total energy usage per household in Sweden. The estimates are made for households with disposable incomes of Skr 9,000, 30,000 and 60,000 in 1969.

such as dwelling insulation and the like, will not suffice in the very long time perspective. And this changing of the consumption pattern is bound to victimize first and foremost those who are now heavy energy consumers, high-income earners. One conceivable way of bringing this about would be via across-the-board methods, such as lowering the rate of increase in real wages or exerting selective leverage on the energy-intensive parts of the consumption pattern. Here we are chiefly thinking of housing, transportation, and energy-intensive parts of the leisure sector (for example, chartered flights and fast-running motorboats). If we take the talk of zero growth in earnest, it is doubtful whether such a policy can be avoided.

Summing up, we think a limited rate of increase in energy usage a) does not pose any threat to employment; b) leads to a restriction on the rate of increase in private consumption, which will intensify the discussion of how the annual increase should be allocated; and c) will lead to a discussion of various ways to sever the direct relation between real income and energy usage, especially for the well-off. One should therefore study how different consumption patterns (housing standard, leisure habits, traveling habits) affect the consumption of energy.

Attention should be called to some general limitations in this analysis. We have taken for granted that continued economic growth is both desirable and possible. We have neglected completely the vital discussion of the connections between real wages and welfare. Besides, it has been assumed that the energy supply will not entail problems which in turn lead to reduced pressure for economic growth. Naturally, it is not all certain that this is really the case. A series of consequences ensuing from economic growth and the clamor for constantly increasing labor productivity may very well lead to attaching ever heavier weight to aspects of welfare other than the purely materialistic ones. To illustrate, we can mention the organization of working life, the jettisoning process (labor-shedding and the like), the demand to curtail the speed of structural change, and the demand to increase our independence and autonomy, above all vis-à-vis other industrialized nations. An important aspect has to do with future employment policy. What we mean by employment and how we evaluate jobs of different kinds have undergone gradual changes during the twentieth century, and there is every reason to suppose that this shifting will continue. For energy purposes this observation has two interesting aspects. First, asking the labor market to meet exacting amenity criteria can affect productivity development and hence the movement of real wages. Second, there seem to be connections between how an individual experiences his work and the type of consumption pattern he chooses. It follows that a gradually changed policy towards working life can also affect the consumption mix.

So one should by no means rule out the possibility that lowering the rate of increase in real wages as part of a vigorously pursued energy-conserving policy will probably not be felt as a loss of welfare. Perhaps the slow rise in real wages will come anyway—as a consequence of attaching ever greater importance to the nonmaterial cravings: more time for the children, better working conditions, better care of the sick and elderly, more opportunities for rotating jobs with leisure time and education, and so forth. Signs of such a development are fully visible as such—but there are also plenty of signs which point in a diametrically opposed direction.

Energy and Environment

Environment and energy interact in several ways. For instance, energy production gives rise to environmental disturbances—sulfur fallout is one example—and environmental protection and clean-up measures draw energy in their turn.

The growing interest of the community at large in *working environment* questions leads to consequences for energy requirements. A recent Secretariat report investigates the energy needed to improve the working environment over a ten-year period. It will be feasible over the longer term to build environmental measures into new production systems, and in that case it is scarcely possible to state which energy usage can be attributed to the demands for a good working environment.

Measures to improve ventilation are utterly dominant for purposes of assessing the energy requirement for a better working environment. The need for energy to mechanize heavy lifting, screenings, and enclosures is insignificant by comparison. Other measures, among them better illumination and automation, can even reduce energy requirements. But here again the effects are relatively small.

If the use of conventional techniques to heat ventilating air carries over into 1985, it would require fuel equivalent to 2 to 3 million tons of oil per annum. That represents about 10 percent of Swedish oil consumption. Since substantial amounts of energy are even now used to heat ventilating air, the increase to 1985 forms but one part of the stated figure.

Nonetheless, there are vast potentials for saving fuel (oil). The installation of heat exchangers and possible utilization of solar heat, together with increased use of waste heat and combustible waste, can reduce oil requirements to under half, or less than 1.5 million tons.

Measures to achieve these savings must be taken now. During the next ten-year period considerable funds will be invested in the working-environment field—which is all the more reason to build in measures from the very outset which lessen the need to provide the new plants with energy in the form of oil. It is therefore important to get to work immediately on overhauling technical standards and economic rules to ensure that these investments are actually carried out.

An increased need for spot ventilation implies that the annual requirement of electric energy for the working environment will double up to 1985. The annual electric energy requirement is estimated to go up by 2.5 to 4.5 TWh to 1985. There are small chances of reducing the expected need for electric energy with economizing measures.

Working environment and energy meet at another point: the environment at workplaces for energy production. To illustrate, some fairly sizable problems are to be found in connection with the extraction of fossil fuels and the mining of uranium, not to mention those foreseen in connection with reprocessing plants. Indeed, problems of the working environment are likely to bulk heavily in the cost calculus of future technologies and might even preclude the exploitation of a specific technology.

Measures on behalf of *external environmental protection* (i.e., outside the job world) likewise draw energy. Table 7 shows where the greatest energy needs may be expected to lie, given the thrust that environmental protection is now taking.

As is evident from the table, the energy required for environmental protection will probably make up a limited part of Swedish energy usage (about 2 to 4 percent) in the coming decade.

If trends continue, something will have to be done about substances and activities whose noxious effects are not discovered until they have become widespread. In that case a policy for protecting the environment amounts to rectifying mistakes after the fact, which is all too likely to engender substantial energy requirements. However, a development which defers to environmental considerations at an early stage, for instance in the planning of a process, can reduce these requirements appreciably compared with the taking of measures ex post facto.

Options are thus available. A case in point is the air pollution caused by motor vehicles. The question of how much energy is consumed in order to clean car exhausts will depend primarily on techniques for cleaning and techniques for engine design. But these technical properties depend in turn on what properties the car engines have. We can reduce the conflicts between energy management and environment by changing such things as engine power, acceleration capacity, and driving characteristics. In other words, there is no absolute connection between fuel consumption and exhaust emission cleaning.

The Volvo Company has developed a method which is reported to lower an automobile's fuel requirement at the same time that the exhaust gases meet exacting specifications. So, if such a technique comes into general use, the 5 to 7 TWh per annum set out in table 7 will disappear by 1985 and result in a net energy saving. Obviously, the technique used matters very much for future energy requirements within the air treatment sector.

Another possibility is replacement of gasoline with methanol, which requires only relatively small changes in engine designs. Methanol makes exhaust gases much cleaner, largely because no lead need be added.

Production of energy has several environmental consequences. Sulfur emissions produced by the combustion of fossil fuels acidify land and water, a now-familiar phenomenon. Heavy

TABLE 7
Estimated Energy Used for Environmental Protection Measures in Sweden,
1975 and 1985 (in TWh)

Direct energy usage to remedy:	Estimated energy used to protect environment in Sweden	
	1975 TWh	1985 TWh
Air pollution		
— from plants	2.8	9—11
— from vehicles	0	5—7
Water polution	0.8	1
Solid waste		
— if energy not recovered	0.08	(0.1-0.2)
— if energy recovered, energy gain	0	—5
Total, direct energy usage	3.7	9—14
Indirect energy usage (investments in pollution control devices)	4—5	4—5
Total, Swedish energy usage	c. 410	c. 525

metals, oil spills, and hydrocarbons are examples of other emissions connected with the use of fossil fuels.

As figure 1 shows, man accounts for a small part of the energy flow on earth. For that reason the climatic effects today are chiefly limited to local effects.

Carbon dioxide is emitted in the course of combustion, too. As a result the content of carbon dioxide is slowly built up in the atmosphere. Carbon dioxide absorbs heat radiation from the earth, which acts to heat up the atmosphere. The possible effects of this heating are the subject of a keenly waged scientific debate. Among these possible effects is melting of floating Arctic ice, which probably would not freeze again afterwards, and the shifting of climate zones with consequences for agriculture.

A combustion of measurable amounts of fossil fuels (oil, gas, coal) leads to carbon dioxide releases on a scale deemed capable of affecting climate considerably. In practice, the chances of cleaning off the carbon dioxide are very small. All told, the world contains greater reserves of fossil fuels than those that can be burned for climatic reasons.

Herein lies an interesting corollary question with ties to foreign policy. If now fears are confirmed, how are international institutions to be built which see to it that the total consumption of fossil fuels does not go out of sight? How is the right to consume fossil fuels to be apportioned? Among large and small countries? Among rich and poor countries? Many questions will remain even after the scientific ones are answered. The problems are illustrated by the United Nations-sponsored deliberations aimed at formulating environmental conventions, for instance on the law of the sea.

To sum up, measures on behalf of the external and internal environment require limited amounts of energy. The desire to improve our environment need not be circumscribed by a desire to curtail the rate of increase in energy usage. No stronger conflict of goals is involved here. By contrast, there are conflicts between energy and environmental policy in the field of energy production. The conflicts may become so strong as to necessitate limiting the production of energy and hence its use. That is one of the reasons why we think it important to create freedom of action in the choice of the next generation of energy sources.

Energy and Geographic Structure

Historically there is a clear-cut connection between a society's energy supply techniques and its geographic structure. A more detailed discussion of the role played by the energy supply system for Sweden's geographic structure is pursued in a recent Secretariat study, where three phases are roughly distinguished:

The *industrialization phase* denoted changing over from an agrarian society to one increasingly based on manufacturing. The effect of this transition was to concentrate workplaces and redistribute human habitation. A pattern of urban settlements emerged based on the new industries as well as a transport system based on railways. The organization and technology embodied in the energy supply system imposed a clear limitation on how this urban pattern evolved. Coal dominated along the coasts and partly along the railways; at other places industries sprang up next to existing—and less movable—energy sources such as falling water or wood. In that way the emerging urban pattern was affected by the locally available energy sources.

The *urbanization phase,* ushered in at about the turn of the century, signified that the urban settlements established in the earlier phase grew at the expense of the agrarian society. Here urban development steers the energy supply, which is based more and more on easy-to-move energy forms such as oil and electricity. In that way the siting of plants becomes less and less dependent on local energy sources. Hence energy supply no longer limits the growth of urban settlements.

The *regionalization phase* was largely ushered in during the 1950s and contains two partly contradictory tendencies. On the one hand the population is converging more and more on Sweden's three metropolitan areas (Stockholm, Göteborg, and Malmö), on the other hand these areas are being split up more and more into large centers with residential, service-providing, and employment facilities. Large distances are bridged by speedy and flexible transport equipment, chiefly the private passenger car. Building coverage spreads out more and more and sets ever greater store by easily transportable energy forms. Oil and electricity increasingly dominate.

In the context of energy, the regionalization process may be described as increasing the need for high-quality energy. Only the energy forms which are very easy to move can be used with present-day technology in those transport systems or those spread-out residential patterns.

Today's urban and regional planning and organizational configuration steer tomorrow's geographic patterns. The discussion also shows that there is a clear, albeit hard-to-analyze, connection between energy supply and geographic structure.

Moreover, energy and land use have an energy/production dimension. Land must be set aside for installations of different kinds. For example, our present power-line corridors lay claim to sizable acreages. In a future energy supply alternative that amply accommodates renewable energy sources, the energy sector will lay greater claim to land, resulting in conflicts with other major land users, the forest industry in particular.

As mentioned earlier, around 1 TWh a year of solar energy radiates on every square kilometer (km^2) of our country. Sweden's energy conversion balances at slightly more than 400 TWh. With a collection technique which has an efficiency rate of 2 percent (annual mean), 20,000 km^2 would then be required to cope entirely with the country's energy supply. That comes to about 5 percent of the land area or about 10 percent of the forested acreage, which will put us in conflict with other land uses if we want to base a large part of the Swedish energy supply on renewable energy sources.

Let us illustrate a trade-off situation which touches on Swedish land use: energy supply and the balance of payments. We choose this example because it is sometimes contended that we must increase our exports in order to manage oil imports. In recent years the balance of payments has become a troublesome problem due to the soaring oil prices. These prices are expected to go on rising. In 1974 oil imports cost about Skr 12,000 million. Thanks to photosynthesis and the like, our forests collect one part of the continuous energy flow. Net production today is about

10 MWh per hectare (ha) and per year. Through more intensive cultivation (pasture, coppice, and so forth) productivity might increase to 100 MWh/ha and per year (0.01 TWh/km^2). (Some studies indicate even higher values.) But suppose, for the sake of this example, that the figure is reasonable. Half the oil consumption will then be tantamount to drawing upon about 7 percent of the forest acreage (or about 1,600,000 ha) for this energy cultivation. The most likely places for this purpose would appear to be abandoned farmland and certain marshes, together totaling perhaps as much as 1,000,000 ha. But if we assume that the whole cultivation supersedes traditional forest production on its present lands, that would reduce exports of forest products by about 10 percent or the equivalent of about Skr 2,000 million. The oil import reduction comes to about Skr 6,000 million. If we were to make use of our land area to produce energy instead of importing oil, that would, if anything, improve the balance of payments, not to mention the obvious advantages accruing in abated emission of sulfur and heavy metals plus a reduced dependence on oil deliveries. Although the numerical reckoning in the example is admittedly on the rough side, it does illustrate that it may be dubious in the long run to continue the present-day policy of not using the forest as fuel but as raw material for pulp and paper products (which are then exported to pay for the oil imports).

To use raw fiber in this way and not as high-grade feedstock for paper processing poses a tougher trade-off, seen globally. The question of whether we should burn oil and gas or reserve them as raw materials for sophisticated purposes is of the same character. It is hard to figure out where a fair trade-off should be struck in these matters. We therefore conclude that these problems are central to our future energy supply and that they must be studied in greater depth.

Consequently, there is every reason to consider questions of land use in conjunction with energy policy. Since land uses are often tied down for very long periods, such rigid commitments may become an important factor which affects the feasible rate of introduction for techniques requiring vast expanses of surface area.

As yet there is no well-reasoned study of how different energy supply systems can be fitted into different spatial structures. But bearing in mind the very long periods involved in urban and regional planning, it is not unthinkable that we have here one of the more fundamental limits to freedom of action in energy policy.

Energy and Foreign Policy

There are (at least) two visible conflicts in the foreign policy field which bear directly on the design of our energy supply. The first concerns our national independence. As we discussed in chapter 2, we shall have to depend on the rest of the world generally and on the Western industrial countries in particular, all according to how future energy supplies are organized. So here there is a clear-cut conflict between the demand for a sustained standard of material well-being with its attendant use of resources and national independence.

Similarly with respect to the developing world, there is a conflict between the resolve to show international solidarity with poor countries and our need for cheap oil above all, to fuel our own economic progress. It follows that future energy policy toward both the industrialized and developing countries can aggravate already existing conflicts.

We begin by considering the situation of the *developing countries*. Many of them are not only dependent on imported energy commodities such as oil but also use huge quantities of domestic fuels such as wood and cow dung. The latter are usually gathered at the village level and are seldom recorded in official statistics. But the exploitation of these domestic energy sources leads successively to increasingly serious effects such as impoverishment and erosion of the soil. In several areas annual forest growth now falls short of meeting the needs of a rapidly growing population. A continued utilization of wood as fuel, for example, leads to deforestation.

The average Swede in 1972 used seventy-five times as much oil a year as the average Indian and nearly fifty times as much as the average Chinese (who uses more coal, however). The conclusion for oil price is clear: even if the industrialized nations consume a great deal of oil per capita, the total quantities are small compared with what may be consumed one day when the rest of the world industrializes. The price of oil is still low seen from the perspective of the affluent world.

If cheap oil were necessary for our economic progress, it follows that the poor countries would indeed never get on the same track with us. There simply is not enough cheap oil to go around. The poor countries must abstain from a line of development which cries every bit as much for cheap oil as ours has done. To put the case mildly, we have here a highly unstable situation.

What can be said about the developing world's needs for different forms of energy? In Sweden we can discuss different energy types as being of relatively equal merit (oil, gas, electricity, district heating) due to our high technological level. For a developing country, many of these forms are not at all comparable. Several of them require an extensive infrastructure to permit their use (power grids, gas pipelines, and so forth). But it is precisely the problem of many such countries that they do not have a sufficiently developed infrastructure, nor do they have access to the capital required for the job. That in its turn helps to explain why they find it so hard to remove themselves from their underdeveloped state. Oil, however, with its unsurpassed ease of transport and storage, high energy density, and use as a propellant may be just the source of energy that can facilitate growth in these countries.

Much of the oil used in the developing countries goes to transportation, but due to their rudimentary infrastructure these countries are often reduced to using the most energy-extravagant

TABLE 8
GEOGRAPHIC DISTRIBUTION OF THE
WORLD'S ENERGY RESOURCES
(fossil fuels and uranium in
light-water reactors).

	Oil	Energy resources, total
Industrial countries	18%	77%
Developing countries	82%	23%

conveyances (automobiles, trucks, and planes instead of, say, trains and ships).

A discussion of what the developing countries need should be supplemented with a picture of what they have (see table 8). Table 8 conceals the fact that some developing countries have huge resources while others have none at all. Presumably, the differences within the industrial-world and developing-country blocs are just as great as between the blocs.

Summing up, a familiar picture appears. The industrial countries are rapidly consuming the oil that exists in the developing countries. At the same time there are large energy resources in the industrial countries (see table 2). It may be questioned whether energy in the form of oil (liquid fuel) is unnecessary to enable the developing countries to industrialize as we have done in the industrial countries. It is therefore plausible to argue that all faith in the industrialization of the developing countries, in the sense familiar to us today, will be buried at the same rate as the industrial countries consume this finite resource. The only possibility seems to be for them to abstain wilfully from adhering to our line of development.

To be sure, great efforts are being made the world over to produce liquid fuels from coal and other materials, but it seems hard to believe that the industrial countries will export these to the developing countries at a sufficiently low price.

The only thing that could really affect the situation would be for the industrial countries, Sweden among them, to limit their oil consumption deliberately for the benefit of the developing world.

There are no mechanisms today to ensure that oil saved in Sweden will redound to the benefit of the developing countries. But this should be seen as a spur towards trying to create such mechanisms and not as an excuse for not doing anything.

The design of energy supply also ties us to a number of dependencies with other *industrial countries*. Economic growth has not only made us dependent on foreign energy sources, it has also implicated us more and more in an international division of labor. There is scarcely any doubt that the demand to make us less dependent on foreign energy sources will collide with the demand to maintain and perhaps intensify the internationalization of the Swedish economy, which, in its turn, is necessary for our material prosperity. One sort of dependence implies the other.

Now we have not yet pursued any more detailed discussion centering on these matters. Chapter 2, however, called attention to two aspects, which we should like to amplify here with a third.

To what extent can we count on getting access to oil and other sources of energy, under conditions of mounting scarcity? If the trend unfolding on the uranium market offers any parallel perspective, there are grounds to start worrying about a rapid bilateralization of the international oil market. One should not preclude the risk that we shall have to pay for energy imports by granting direct concessions in other aspects of foreign policy. The heaviest factor here, presumably, is the U.S. dependence on imported oil. The American program for self-sufficiency has been a failure so far and oil imports are soaring, especially from the Middle East. Here, moreover, Saudi Arabia is playing more and more of a strategic role. It is not unlikely that the growing import dependence will prevail on powerful American groups to feel compelled to guarantee oil supplies by exerting leverage of one kind or another. That would aggravate the risk not only of oil being sucked into an East-West or a North-South conflict, but also of leading to conflict inside the North-West block (i.e., between the industrial countries, such as the EEC members, Japan, and the United States).

To what extent can we control the utilization of our own energy reserves, uranium in particular? The nuclear fuel cycle is a technical system so vast that intergovernmental agreements must be reached now. It is also an open question whether the foreign dependencies we already have will push us willy-nilly into a breeder economy.

Other interesting dependencies are to be found on the energy-saving side. Many energy-economizing measures make it necessary to change the operating specifications of consumer products such as automobiles and refrigerators. Can we pursue our own policy in this respect? Or will considerations of trade policy force us to adapt to what the big EEC countries claim to be a reasonable policy for saving on energy? For example, can we introduce more rigorous gasoline consumption standards for cars than the EEC has? If the discussion of exhaust gases serves as a guide, problems will be looming ahead. The recycling of materials is another economizing measure that may require altered products. There are also interesting connections between the clamor to remove what are called technical barriers to trade and, say, the organizational structure of the Swedish energy supply system. Thus the manufacturers of consumer durables are striving to get all European countries to adopt the same electric voltage. In Sweden that would lead to upgrading the voltage quality—from 220 V $\pm$ 10 percent to perhaps 230 V $\pm$ 5 percent. Not only would this run up a bigger bill for the electric power provider, but it would also very likely require an organization centralization which in its turn could impede the introduction of new technology.

One question we have not taken up here but which is nonetheless central is whether Swedish industries can pay substantially higher prices for energy than their counterparts abroad. If not, our freedom of action in energy policy could be narrowed. The desire to broaden this latitude would then conflict with the desire to operate an open-door economy.

6
Choice of Energy Carriers and Freedom of Action in Energy Policy

Introduction

WE SHALL NOW go one step further in the analysis of how we can create freedom of action with regard to the renewable-sources alternative.

One critical point in a strategy to increase freedom of action for the renewable alternative is not to use energy of higher quality than is actually necessary to do the work at hand. This is discussed to some extent in chapter 4 ("What types of energy do we need?"). The energy carrier, which links energy producer with energy user, is the critical factor there.

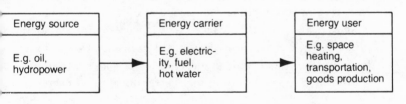

Fig. 10

Switching energy carriers is expensive. We did that earlier in space heating, for example, when we changed over from wood to coal to oil to district heating. Each time, new equipment is required and, to some extent, capital is eroded.

In practice, therefore, the possibility of introducing new energy carriers is tied to the technical equipment the user already has, the rate at which this can be changed, and the extent of that change.

We shall discuss these matters in the present chapter, beginning with an analysis of energy quality. After that we shall discuss energy carriers in very general terms and conclude with a discussion of technical design.

Energy Quality

In chapter 4 we mentioned that different energy carriers—fuel, electricity, hot water, and so forth—vary in quality. As a general rule we can say that the higher the quality, the more diversified usage that is feasible.

The quality of energy may be described as the degree of disorder in the small constituents of matter. When we use energy we transfer it from a well-ordered to a more disordered form. A well-ordered energy form is more valuable than one that is more disordered. Every type of energy can be assigned a "quality index" (entropy) which indicates how disordered it is. For practical purposes it is often sufficient to introduce three classes of energy: extra prime, prime, and second-rate.

Since disorder invariably increases when energy is used, extra prime energy can be easily transmitted in prime or second-rate form. But we cannot, without incurring losses, move in the opposite direction and make extra prime energy out of prime energy.

In an oil furnace used to heat a one-family house, prime energy (chemical energy) is transmitted in second-rate form (hot water).

In a thermal power plant which is oil-fired, three parts of prime energy (chemical energy, measured as kWh) are transmitted to one part extra prime (electricity) and two parts second-rate (waste heat).

TABLE 9
DIFFERENT QUALITY CLASSES OF ENERGY

Extra prime energy	— Gravitation energy — Kinetic energy — Electric energy
Prime energy	— Nuclear energy — Sunlight — Chemical energy — Heat at high temperature
Second-rate energy	— Heat at low temperature (waste heat)

A heat pump can with the aid of one part extra prime (electric) energy and two parts of low-temperature heat from the environment, produce three parts with a somewhat higher temperature, to heat a house, for instance.

A diesel engine converts three parts of prime (chemical energy) to one part extra prime (kinetic energy) and two parts second-rate (waste heat). Waste heat can be used for heating water, and the extra prime energy can run the heat pump above. This then yields an additional three parts of heat since two parts of second-rate are taken from the environment. All told, three parts of prime (chemical) energy are then converted to five parts heat at low temperature.

These examples show that different energy conversion techniques vary in their ability to turn the scarcity factor—energy of prime or extra prime quality—to good account. The examples also show that techniques which utilize prime energy well presuppose more complicated combinations of energy carriers. Both electricity and hot water are examples. Such systems complicate not only the technical but also the organizational design.

Finally, certain energy technologies available in the future can offer brand new possibilities for combining the carriers. One example is hydrogen. Electricity can be converted into hydrogen through electrolysis. Conversely, hydrogen can produce electricity and (waste) heat in a fuel cell. So here again different carriers are combined in a new way.

Let us look at the quality of energy in present usage. Table 10 makes a rough breakdown of the energy qualities needed in Sweden today.

As of 1975 the principal energy carrier was electricity for items 1-3 and oil for items 4-6. Items 1 and 2 will probably continue to be based on electricity in the next few decades, whereas for item 3 other energy carriers may be envisioned. For item 4 as well as for item 5 methanol, for example, can become an alternative. Water and solar heat are conceivable for item 6, where electric heating now plays a growing role.

Process heat (item 5) is chiefly used in the processing industries, such as paper and pulp, iron and steel, cement, and chemicals. These industries use process heat primarily for chemical conversion, for instance iron ore into iron, pulp into paper. Here high temperatures are necessary with present-day technology.

It should now be said that process heat is not a particularly homogeneous concept, but to the best of our knowledge there are no more detailed descriptions available which show how industry's heat requirements are distributed by temperature intervals. There are a number of studies which show that a large part of industry's need for process heat lies in the interval 100-200°C. Solar energy for production of low-grade steam is currently under study in the United States, and it is not impossible that at least part of industry's process heat can be produced in this way.

We find accordingly that about two-fifths of energy usage could tap energy sources of lower quality than those actually being used today—namely, space heating. For the other two heavy items—transporation and process heat—the current scene by and large does not offer any alternative to energy forms of high quality. Of course, there are conservation measures that can be taken which could reduce a specific usage.

TABLE 10
ROUGH BREAKDOWN BY ENERGY QUALITY
OF THE SWEDISH ENERGY BALANCE, 1971.

	Proportions in %			
	Industry	Commun- ications	Other (residen- tial, com- mercial)	Total
1. Electricity for lighting and small motors (in households)	1	0	5	6
2. Electricity for chemical processes (electrolytic)	2	0	0	2
3. Stationary motors mainly in industry)	5	0	1	6
4. Transportation	2	17	0	19
5. Process heat (about 100°C and higher)	25	0	0	25
6. Low-temperature heat (space heating, about 100°C and lower)	6	0	36	42
	41	17	42	100

It is also evident that the electrification level is a central varia-ble of energy policy. There are few applications where electricity is really essential.

The Choice of Energy Carriers

The energy carrier's function is to distribute energy from places and points in time where it is produced to places and points in time where it is used. This means that great importance attaches to the transportability of the energy carrier. The historical development of energy carriers may also be described as a trend toward ever better properties when it comes to energy density, transportability, and storability.

Today's energy systems, with oil as the dominant energy carrier, possess very good properties of storability and transportability. Oil has a high energy density (i.e., recoverable amount of energy per kilogram) and is easy to store. What properties can those energy carriers have which are meant to replace oil?

Alternative energy sources and energy usage can be coupled in various ways. Figure 11 illustrates examples of energy systems having one or three energy carriers.

In Case 1 the energy carrier must be of high quality to be able to satisfy energy conversion processes with varying quality needs. Electricity is such an energy carrier. It lacks storability, which in Sweden today is made up for by generating it with hydropower (water is saved in the power station dam until the energy is needed).

Seen from the user's viewpoint, electricity has a very high degree of flexibility. Connecting to a single socket on the wall enables the user to satisfy many different needs. Standardization of such things as wall sockets, voltages, and number of cycles can hold down the costs of producing electrical equipment.

Seen from the viewpoint of the energy producer—and given today's technology—this user flexibility is matched by a substantial rigidity: long construction periods, big systems, complicated coordinating functions, and so forth. In this case the user's comfort is offset by a high degree of centralization on the production side.

Case 2 can be flexibly designed on the producer side by first designing the user side so that it can take advantage of different energy carriers.

Examples of conceivable energy carriers are hydrogen, methanol, and water. Hydrogen can be produced from water, for instance, in connection with nuclear power. At 800–1,000°C (a higher temperature than in LWR) hydrogen can be produced

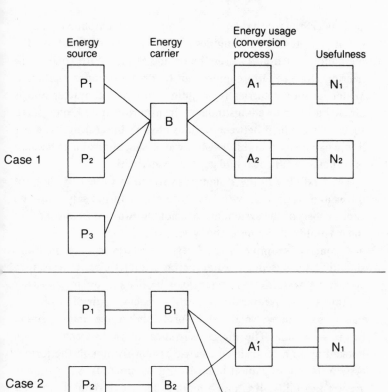

Fig. 11. Two energy systems where flexibility has been created through energy carriers or by designing the user side.

catalytically, that is, with assistance from a chemical substance (catalyst). Hydrogen gas can be moved in gas pipelines, burned for heat production, perhaps stored in metallic hydrates (metal hydrogen compounds), and used in engines. Methanol can be obtained from pyrolysis (dry distillation) of organic material, such as energy forests, and can be mixed with gasoline for application in present-day engines. Lead is then replaced by the methanol, which also raises the octane rating. With small engineering changes Otto engines can be driven on pure methanol. Water as energy carrier is of quite a different character and is already used in dwellings today to transport heat and, on a small scale, to store heat between periods of sunshine. Naturally, every liquid can be used in this way but water is mentioned here because of its high specific heat and general availability.

The flexibility in the system is provided in Case 1 by the producer and in Case 2 by the user of energy. In the same way the capital costs of the system are distributed, with consequences for the feasibility of changing the system.

A concrete example of the foregoing relates to space heating: should it be based on water or on a direct-electric-resistance system? A water-based system can be hooked up to a district heating plant, a centralized electric system, individual oil furnaces, sometimes wood, and—probably in the more remote future—the sun. The direct-resistance alternative can only be hooked up to a centralized electric system. Although the former system is more capital-intensive, it commands substantially greater flexibility. It is much more expensive to rebuild a direct-electric-resistance system into one that is water-heated, for example, than the other way around.

Alternative Energy Systems

Today we use high-grade energy forms for all purposes. For the future we can speak of two main alternatives for the choice of carriers.

The first alternative, which is a sequel to the current situation, signifies that new carriers are of high quality and give the user great flexibility.

Under the second alternative, energy of higher quality than necessary will not be used. It is a thermodynamic adjustment

Energy usage

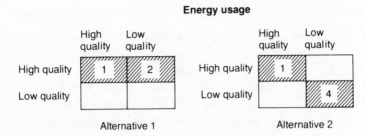

Fig. 12. Alternative energy systems.

between the energy carrier and the process selected by the user to convert energy, where the user's technical system is tailor-made to imposed outside conditions.

In figure 12, alternative 1 corresponds to a future energy supply system based on a high proportion of nuclear power (breeder reactors), perhaps a large proportion of coal for combined power and heating, or some equivalent. The fuel requirement is met with synthetic fuels, produced perhaps by coal and high-temperature reactors. It is harder to see an energy supply system under Alternative 1 based on renewable energy sources, but we can think of one based on forests harvested for their energy content.

Alternative 2 corresponds roughly to an energy supply system based on renewable energy sources which are augmented by certain high-grade sources, such as hydropower (which of course is a renewable source) and methanol (produced perhaps by energy forests) as fuel. At the same time an energy supply system under Alternative 2 can very well be built up with breeder reactors and coal as the energy bases. The sources in Alternative 1 thus fit into Alternative 2, but not necessarily the other way round.

A big difference lies in the role of the national electric system. In the first case it is the very pillar of the country's energy supply, in the latter case the electric system's role is adjunctive, that is, it serves as standby to the renewable sources, which will perforce have to be more locally organized.

One part of a rigid commitment to any one energy supply system lies on the user side. It is by means of measures that are finely tuned both toward energy users and producers that freedom of action is created. Hence a critical factor is the coupling between the two—the energy carrier.

The discussion of different energy carriers can be moved to the technical plane. For each energy carrier there is a system of technical components, interdependent and adapted to one another.

Private motoring can be taken as an example. Passenger cars are powered by gasoline that is produced from oil in refineries. Refineries, distribution systems, and automobile engines are all adapted to one another and supported by a sometimes rather complicated system of rules and regulations. Beyond certain limits one cannot change the fuel before automobile engines have to be readjusted, the servicing requirements changed, the working environment criteria more precisely defined, and so forth.

The electric system is another example. In earlier days there was a plethora of voltages, frequencies of cycles, and so on. Inner Stockholm had direct current right down to the 1960s. Today, the whole system from waterfalls to refrigerators is adapted to a specific mains voltage, a specific frequency of cycles, and so forth. A large part of the invested capital also lies on the user side in all the appliances and machines which households and enterprises have. New components must be designed so that they can exist alongside the old ones.

In practice, therefore, the introduction of new energy carriers makes it necessary to adapt equipment, heating systems, appliances, motors, and engines accordingly. It stands to reason that these adaptations may incur heavy costs. Besides, the examples with electric heating prove that it is much cheaper to switch from water as energy carrier for space heating to electricity than vice versa.

So the resistance raised against new energy carriers—whether it be economic or not—very much depends on how easy it is to adapt existing equipment on the premises of energy users and distributors to the new carrier. To the best of our knowledge this type of implementation problem has not yet been systematically discussed.

We should like to point out, however, that new energy carriers are a matter of synchronous adjustment by energy producer and equipment producer. Today, automobile engines (and repair shops) are geared to the products put out by the refineries and vice versa. The same thing goes for refrigerators vis-à-vis the performance criteria required by the electricity producers.

It follows that energy producers, energy users, and equipment producers must be affected at the same time when new energy carriers are to be introduced. The adjustments involved are now handled in great measure by various trade associations, such as the Swedish Association of Electricity Supply Undertakings. Such decisions will now become strategic.

On this level, therefore, a strategy for increased freedom of action on behalf of the renewable sources contains the following components:
— the energy carrier chosen must be usable both in a renewable and a coal and/or breeder solution;
— energy usage must husband the scarce factor, energy of high quality;
— the electrification level is to be held back;
— the array of energy carriers will probably have to be a compromise between the two solutions;
— at the same time this array of carriers should be flexibly introducible compatible with existing equipment on the users' premises.

7
Energy and Social Organization

Introduction

WE ALREADY observed by way of introduction (chapter 1) that an energy policy for freedom of action will impose partly new demands on the legislative and executive branches of government (Parliament and Cabinet). Above all it will entail a change in the division of responsibilities between politically representative assemblies and various private and public producer interests.

Such an energy policy will require measures to restrain the rate of increase in energy usage in general and the use of high-quality energy in particular.

However, a policy of this kind has not only a technical and an economic dimension but an organizational one as well. A program for housing insulation, for example, will impose other demands on the construction industry and its organization compared with, say, a house-building program. To preserve waste heat from the processing industry and utilize it in district heating systems will impose new demands on forms of collaboration between local authorities and business firms. Gasoline-thrifty cars are not only a technical problem but perhaps also an institutional one, as exemplified domestically by the organization of the engineering sector (automobile manufacturing, automotive services) and internationally (can we have other rules and regulations for energy usage than, say, the EEC countries?).

If we are fired by an ambition to economize on materials and transportation, the organizational and institutional complexity is likely to increase. Economizing on materials is very much a matter of logistics, of steering material flows (systems which today are not steered at all in the first place) and product design. As for economizing on transportation, that also has a great deal to do with the organizational structure of society.

There is scarcely any doubt that an energy policy which is based on economizing on energy in general and energy of high quality in particular will put a premium on organizational and institutional ingenuity. In this chapter we shall confine ourselves to looking at one special aspect, namely the organization of energy supply itself, and ask whether this system as it is now structured poses an obstacle to a renewable alternative.

We shall therefore develop a number of ideas about which instrumentalities are available to Parliament and Cabinet for steering the process of technical change within the energy sphere. But even now we can observe that the interest shown in central government's role in that respect seems to have been extremely limited. These words are uttered as a caveat to explain why parts of this chapter are rather hypothetical and groping.

The chapter starts off with a few words about different attitudes to or ways of looking at technical change. From this we draw a number of conclusions, which we then illustrate with a longer example taken from the selection of technology within the Swedish electricity sector. After that the conclusions are elaborated and we arrive at the possibilities that Parliament and Cabinet have for steering the technical change. Finally, we present some ideas on how the demand for increased freedom of action can be translated into organizational terms.

The Dynamics of Technical Change: Some Attitudes About How Technologies are Chosen

There is a fairly copious literature on the driving forces behind technical change, representing various perspectives. Our aim here is to find a perspective that is suited to our problem: namely, a perspective that can be used to show how to steer by democratic means—via political processes in representative assemblies—the process of technical change unfolding in a certain field. Such an angle of vision must dwell on the roles played by representative assemblies—the municipal councils, the county councils/county administrative boards, and Parliament—namely, a) to allocate economic resources and b) to steer by way of legislation the division of responsibilities among "constituents," that is, different parties with interests in the society. It is the latter aspect in particular that we are going to take up.

With that we are forced to choose an angle of approach divergent from the one existing literature provides. We can make some headway, however, by picking out fragments from the literature concerned with organization theory, political science, and economics.

The economic literature (especially that dealing with political economy) usually points up the importance of profitability for technical change. The only new technical components introduced are those which pay off on commercial grounds. The ranks of organization theorists, moreover, include those who contend that every technical system is interwoven in a social system, where the component individuals, their roles, work tasks, cooperation patterns, mutual relations, and so forth largely depend precisely on the (production) technology in question. Hence technical change does not only imply increased microeconomic profitability; it also implies a threat to the existing social organization. The consequence will be to favor that technical change which least disturbs the existing social pattern at a workplace, firm, or government agency. It follows that the opposition to new technology must be acknowledged as a reality and thus enter into our conception.

But in addition a broader perspective must be adopted than that provided by theories of the firm and other organizations. As we have repeatedly argued, the technical systems we are discussing are not limited to any one organization. On the contrary, the whole chain from the waterfall to the flatiron must be seen as a single technical system—*but* with many different organizations involved.

Then the profitability of one or another new technical component for any one organization—the firm, agency, or household—will be dependent on the division of responsibilities in force. And here a central role is played by Parliament and Cabinet (and flowing from this, the political science and sociology of law philosophies). That is because it is Parliament and Cabinet who, directly or indirectly, determine the division of responsibilities between producers and distributors, between these and consumers, and so forth. The price of electricity for consumers depends, for instance, on the level of interest rates, the terms of loans, the depreciation rules which hold for municipal companies and for government agencies, and on the rules governing the state's capital fund. But, the price also depends on what claims for damages for, say, trespass on land shall accrue to the landowner where a hydropower plant is located. Additionally, there are those rules which regulate, for example, how rigorous the safety and security standards are on nuclear power, on its waste management, and what environmental hazards are acceptable when oil or coal are used. So the microeconomic profitability for one or another organization is highly dependent on a complicated system of rules, a system for which Parliament and Cabinet are responsible, directly and indirectly.

As we mentioned earlier, we have also superimposed on the technical system "from waterfall to flatiron" a constellation of interest groups (electricity producers, appliance producers, and others) which extends beyond the individual firm and often cuts straight across public and private interests. The fact that technical change shifts the distribution of powers is valid not only within individual firms, it also holds for the community at large.

Accordingly we take the following ideas as starting points for the discussion of how Parliament and Cabinet can steer technical change:

— The criterion of private profitability derived from managerial economics bears crucially upon whether or not to introduce a new technology.

— This profitability is dependent in turn on a set of rules which

among other things define the division of responsibilities—
who is to decide over what—and for which Parliament and
Cabinet are directly and indirectly responsible.

— But the introduction of new technology also bumps up against
barriers and opposition within firms and organizations which
chiefly originate in demands to retain existing social patterns.

— This opposition has its counterpart in those power groupings
and often powerful interests which encircle every technical
system in society.

By way of illustration take the evolution of the Swedish electricity
supply system from the end of the nineteenth century to the
present time. Our main thesis is that there is a very strong connection between the organizational and the technical designs of
the electricity supply system.

Technical and Organizational Change: Example from the Electricity Sector

Seen from the international outlook, the Swedish electricity supply system bears a somewhat distinctive stamp. First of all, the
retail distribution of electricity—that is, all the way to the end
consumer—is separated from its production. Second, a pattern
of intimate collaboration has evolved between different private
and public (above all the State Power Board) producers of electricity.

This organizational structure, which meant a great deal for the
time when nuclear power was introduced in Sweden, has its roots
in nineteenth-century technology. Swedish electricity production
was at first coal-based. Electric power was generated by private
and municipal companies, above all in the cities, and was distributed by these same firms. Consistent use was made of direct
current, since this permitted lower transmission cost for the same
voltage than alternating current. With that a number of local
monopolies were also created.

Long-distance transportation of electricity via alternating
current became feasible toward the end of the nineteenth century.

Two consequences ensued: first, it became possible to use hydro-power for electricity generation; second, the local monopolies were broken. (The technical background: it is cheaper to transport electric energy at high than at low voltages. At the same time this presupposes upward and downward transformations into different voltage levels, which in its turn presupposes alternating current.)

Hydropower was not exploited overnight. The ruling legislation first had to be changed. The first step was the law of 1902 which entitled electric power producers to draw power lines over land owned by others. Step two was the twenty-year period of legislative work required to amend the Water Act, which presupposed that riparian owners would agree on an expansion, which of course impeded the negotiating process. The new Water Act, which for all practical purposes allowed private expropriation of land, was backed up by powerful industrial interests.

An interesting side commentary is that the introduction of a new technology here required not only new legislation—that is, active intervention by Parliament and Cabinet—but also wrought rather far-reaching changes in the attitude to private ownership of property.

The advent of the Water Act triggered a rapid expansion of hydropower. Many producers tried to protect their local monopoly by choosing more or less odd voltages and/or cycle counts, and what appeared on the surface to be a fight over purely technical details was actually more concerned with the question of who would wield dominion over the future course of events. The uniform adoption of 220-V voltage and 50 cycles per second prepared the ground for lowered costs, notably by way of an increased coordination, which in its turn was conducive to the concentration of authority.

The 1920s can be characterized by the struggle among hydropower producers over stretches of falling water. Bit by bit the old coal-fired power plants changed over to buying current, but they held on to the distribution right. Much of the electricity in rural areas was distributed by cooperative societies, who more often than not would be furnished with capital by the electrical power producers.

So a system emerged during the 1930s which may be characterized by segregation of producers from distributors and by a great many producers operating independently of one another. More and more joint ventures were contracted between these parties, and a big fight between the private electricity producers and the State Power Board broke out in the late 1930s. That fight was about who should control the transmission of electric energy from northern to southern Sweden. It was not settled until 1946, when the Government granted the State Power Board the sole and exclusive right to build and run the trunk grid.

Another consequence was to permit merged runs between different power producers, which led to building up a very complicated system of contracts. Gradually the State Power Board increased its dominance, and towards the end of the 1950s one can just about say that the production of electricity was nationalized from the operational aspect. But not so from the ownership aspect.

The mechanisms behind this dominance are of themselves interesting examples of the interplay between technology and legislation. A critical point turned out to be the identity of who would be put in charge of the transformer stations at the terminals of the trunk grid.

The 1950s witnessed a hardening debate on the future expansion of hydropower, and partly for environmental reasons many persons began to look around for new electricity production alternatives. There were two, namely, thermal power (either nuclear power or fossil-fueled) or combined generation. The former was confined to electricity generation alone, the latter combined electricity generation with the production of hot water for district heating (i.e., heat piped in from some central plant to a group of buildings). Thermal power suited the electricity producers; cogeneration suited those cities which distributed electric power and expanded district heating. The combined generation technology enabled the cities and the electricity distributors to make themselves partly independent, and a cartel of these distributors became a real threat to the electric power producers.

The development of nuclear power is interesting here. It was first justified in Sweden on grounds that fuel would be saved and oil imports reduced—indeed, the initial proposals provided for atomic heating plants. Gradually interest began to shift towards combined electricity and heat production, and a project for this purpose was also completed (Ågesta). However, the development in the United States was solely based on electricity-producing light-water reactors (which in their turn had been spun off from the nuclear submarine program) and these reactors were the first to be offered commercially.

One reason for the success of the light-water reactors was that this was the reactor type which required the least adjustment of the organizational structure then existing in the United States. Since this country did not have any market for district heating, out-and-out electricity production was the only application for nuclear power. Besides, the policy of the Atomic Energy Commission was to divide up the nuclear fuel cycle among different private firms, so the utility companies did not have to worry about components of the fuel cycle other than the reactor itself. Obviously, this facilitated the introduction of a new and complicated technology, but it also meant that the other parts of the fuel cycle— mainly reprocessing and waste management—would not be developed at the same rate.

The 1960s can be said to mark the acme (so far) of the struggle for supremacy between producers and distributors. This fight was triggered when plans to build a combined nuclear-power and heating plant in Västerås were called off, whereupon the city authorities decided to build their own facility based on oil. A long string of cities were ready to start any minute after Västerås. A vigorous build-up of combined power and heating plants would permit many cities to switch over from buying electricity to producing it themselves and perhaps even selling it to other distributors. This threatened the rate of expansion for nuclear power—the alternative cherished by the electricity producers—besides which these producers would have to assume quite another role: they would have had to concentrate on supplying the electricity distributors with stand-by power, smoothing out peak loads, and so forth. The dominance wielded by the electricity producers over their environment would diminish at the same rate as the electricity distribution increased their independence.

Many weapons were deployed in this fight. One was the 1963 tariff reform, which was aimed directly at neutralizing the distributor cartel. At the time the rates applied to bulk consumers were reduced also.

By and large, the end result of the fight was that the State Power Board—as standard-bearer for the electricity producers—shattered the distributor cartel but accepted combined power and heating plants for the vision of technological progress they embodied. However, the terms of expansion and, above all, of operations are very much dictated by the electricity producers. There are many ways of devising rules to control the profit performance of combined power and heating plants.

Looking back, it is interesting to note that the drama of struggle over technology choice for future electric power production was mainly enacted outside the arena of political debate. No more than scant accounts are to be found in the pages of official government reports, bills, parliamentary papers, and the like.

A fairly straight line can be traced from the early expansion of hydropower, the state's involvement in that expansion, and thence, by way of trunk-grid conflicts and merged runs, to the Swedish nuclear power program. Gradual legal changes and homogenizations of technical equipment, rate-setting, and so on, helped to cut costs, but in addition the producers, who were fragmented at first, were welded together into one bloc.

What, then, was the system of rules which made it possible to bring out power plus heat as an alternative to nuclear power? First of all, it was the fact that the cities were not only distributors of electricity but also bore the responsibility for expansion of district heating, which in its turn was based on their involvement in urban and regional planning.

One can say, perhaps a little crudely, that the nuclear power alternative was a logical consequence of developing the electricity sector, whereas combined generation was a technology which happened to fit well into the areas of responsibility which Swedish cities had assumed during the 1950s.

Now what can this development illuminate? That the division of responsibilities not only between electricity producers and distributors of district heating and electric power but also between energy suppliers and users has the paramount role in this picture; that components of the rules system, such as the obligation to deliver, licensing regulations, and scheduling tariff rates, form major ingredients in the picture too.

The equipment producer should also be mentioned. The expansion of electricity usage assumes that there are electric appliances to buy, and here there are interesting connections not only between appliance producers and electric power suppliers (e.g., what voltage variations one can accept) but also between appliance producers and consumers.

Take consumer durables such as refrigerators and kitchen ranges. In some countries these goods are owned by the energy producers (the utilities). The closest counterpart in Sweden would appear to be the National Telecommunications Administration, which owns the telephones installed in households. In other countries individual households own their own kitchen equipment. Under the system of rules devised in Sweden, the landlords provide this equipment while central government helps out with the financing on the strength of the housing loan ordinance. The principles which govern the amending of this statute also contain a built-in expansion factor for such items as consumer durables, and hence for the capital-goods producers and for the energy sector.

In addition to the role that the division of responsibilities plays in the introduction of one technology and not the other, we wish to single out the role of organizational inertia (dynamic conservatism). It is obvious, for example, that electricity producers prefer a technology of a kind that will preserve this role for them and will therefore work against any technology that might tie them together with other systems such as heating. The desire—call it the compulsion—to dominate one's environment and reduce uncertainties runs through every organization. To illustrate again with electricity producers: they want to have control (though not necessarily official control) over the electricity distributors. The same thing obviously holds for the oil companies. There is no doubt that these enterprises will have great importance in choosing, say, which propulsion system can supplant the gasoline engine in the automobile.

Indeed, one can predict that technology which interconnects such disparate systems—combining electricity and heat production—will come up against much greater opposition than technology which lies wholly within one or the other production chain. This takes on special significance if we wish to save energy of high quality. That is because we would be systematically forced into a coupling of electricity with heat, electrical fuel with waste heat (fuel cells), and so forth.

Finally, along with the division of responsibilities and organizational dynamics—which evidently hang together—we should like to point up the importance of patterns of expectations. If electricity producers manage to persuade users that electricity will continue to remain cheap, then the market for electric power will grow. With that the economies of scale can be exploited, which increases the probability that prices will remain low. By the same token, the market for combined power and heating plants is dependent on the settlement pattern, which in its turn depends on what the urban and regional planners think about which types of housing people want.

Incidentally, a similar development holds for the heating of dwelling units. Electric heat was gradually introduced during the 1960s, it being assumed that dwellings could be heated cheaply and over large areas of floor space.

But is is also obvious that these patterns of expectations are stimulated and perhaps also formulated by powerful producer interests, who want to create a market for their future products.

Expansion: Is it Built in?

The electricity sector's expansion since the turn of the century has been phenomenal. At the same time the price of electricity has fallen. Here again, of course, there is a connection between these two developments.

To what extent was this expansion facilitated by (or did it hinge on) the design of the system of rules and the division of responsibilities); and conversely, to what extent is the expansion necessary for the component organizations given the present rules?

The discussion in this section concerns itself not only with energy producers (P) but also with energy consumers (C) and appliance producers (A). Among these three there are distinct conventions crucial for expansion. To illustrate:

— between P and C: obligation to deliver, scheduling of tariff rates,
— between C and A: financing terms, ownership,
— between P and A: standards for voltage stability.

Added to the foregoing, of course, is a raft of other customs concerning how the producer should behave. Probably the most important of these calls upon the producer to bear his own costs.

We pointed out in the previous section the effect that ownership of consumer durables has on the rate of expansion. It is most likely that this rate would have been lower if the tenants themselves had owned the equipment, which is the case in certain other countries.

Nowadays the landlord is responsible for the electric wiring on his property. But that's not the way it was in the past. In the early twentieth century the landlord's responsibility was restricted to providing only one outlet in the apartment—assuming the apartment had been wired in the first place—after which it was up to the tenant to equip himself with extension cords to different rooms. The idea that the responsibility for more adequate apartment wiring should pass over from tenant to landlord came about as a way of facilitating the expansion of electricity at a time when demand fell as power-efficient metal filament bulbs replaced carbon-filament ones.

This type of discussion has more than mere historical interest: it will surface anew on the day when fuel cells will be sufficiently cheap to be used at the residential level. There is no doubt but that this will affect the expansion rate. But who will then own the equipment: the electric power company, the gas company (hydrogen producer), the tenant, or the landlord?

There are also interesting connections between appliance producers and energy producers. Today's A.C. voltage delivers about 50 cycles per second (varying only within permissible limits). The electricity supply sector has undertaken to maintain this quality, and the appliance producers have adapted themselves accordingly. For instance, major frequency oscillations would disrupt the running of papermaking machinery, ruining the paper. This frequency stabilization is a pretty easy task for today's hydropower-based systems.

But demands for voltage and frequency stability, which might look reasonable in a hydropower-based and/or nuclear-power-based system, are not self-evidently reasonable if, say, we want to introduce large amounts of wind power. This would presumably increase the cost of maintaining quality—and in so doing increase the costs of wind power compared, for instance, with the costs of nuclear power. However, it might well be that quality is needed by only a small number of consumers. Perhaps it is more reasonable to introduce wind power and accept lower quality, forcing those consumers who cannot dispense with high quality to underwrite the extra cost of obtaining suitable equipment themselves.

Thus it can be seen that quality demands which appear natural and well-justified in the light of a particular energy technology may actually be quite unreasonable in light of some others. Quality demands might also pose obstacles to technical change.

The most important component in the system of rules, however, is the setting of tariffs. And there is no doubt that this process has sought primarily to stimulate the increased consumption of electricity.

The following passage, quoted from the Swedish periodical *Teknisk Tidskrift* (1919), well summarizes both the hitherto existing and subsequent tariff-rate policy: ". . . no matter how the tariffs are structured, the goal for a rational tariff is and will remain not only to make sure of giving the power supplier that compensation which is required to cover his costs, but also to promote as far as possible an intensive use of electric energy for all those various purposes which may come into question. This is actually to the benefit not only of the supplier but also of the consumer and last but not least to the country as a whole."

Earlier tariff rates, for instance, had either a low fixed cost or none at all but a high variable cost. This made it cheap to hook up to the power grid and to use only a little electricity for such things as lighting. After that rate setting was gradually changed so as to increase the fixed cost and reduce the variable cost. The obvious result was to favor usage among those who were already connected. The theoretical motivation for this rate structure came later: it was said to be geared to the cost structure of the electricity sector.

More recently, the rate-setting process has also come into use as an instrument for fending off other production alternatives (first and foremost municipal back pressure).

Finally, it should be pointed out that the setting of rates within the electricity sector gradually has become more and more dominated by the State Power Board; furthermore the Board is the only public trading agency which does not have to submit its rate changes to the government for approval.

Along with the rules and the rates structure, there is yet another aspect of the electric power sector that is worth stressing. That is the sector's ability to adapt itself to (unforeseen) changes in demand.

The electricity sector is characterized by long planning times and large indivisibilities. Consequentially, capital-expenditure decisions must be made with reference to forecasts of how demand for electric power is going to develop over perhaps a ten-year period. The forecasts and the capital investment costs are used to calculate (and successively adjust) the rate or price to be charged. If everything comes true, all well and good. But if demand is overestimated, the given rate will not suffice to bring in the revenues needed to finance investments. If any one capital-outlay project can then be postponed, all well and good. Failing this (postponing is hard to do in view of the big projects involved) rates will have to be raised, and as a consequence demand may work out even lower than the forecast figures. In the long run, the electricity sector runs a clear risk of ending up in financial crises under these circumstances; put simply, consumers are able to adapt more rapidly to price changes than producers are able to adapt to consumers. The net result might well be a vicious circle, and the cure is to try to prop up demand at the very level envisioned with the expansion programs. That can be done in various ways: by advertising, information campaigns, pressuring appliance producers.

The electric utility companies in the United States have partly wound up in this situation. Water supply in Sweden, which has the same type of cost structure, is beset with similar problems in some municipalities. District heating systems in different municipalities could end up there.

Inflexible production systems pose a big problem. A vigorous commitment to energy-saving technologies could put the electricity producers above all into a predicament, considering that raising tariff rates is the only way to cope with a contingent period of changing over to a lower investment rate. But the rate increase strengthens the incentive to save energy.

Now what can be done about this? The American utilities have responded, at least in part, by backing up electricity generation with shorter lead times: coal-fired plants instead of nuclear power, oil-fired plants instead of coal, and so forth. As a result electricity prices have gone higher, but so has adaptability.

The problem becomes more perplexing the more inflexible the production apparatus is. And a trend towards a coal and/or breeder technology would undoubtedly increase this rigidity. It is not certain that the same would hold for a renewable-sources solution, since the time taken to build the individual projects is so much shorter and with that the ability to adapt to the market's variations is greater.

The inference to be drawn from this line of reasoning, which is admittedly vague, is that it may be necessary to investigate whether today's expansion-oriented system of rules and regulations will not have to be modified if a renewable-sources solution is to be introduced.

Organizations and Uncertainty

One of our basic premises has been that the introduction of new technology must be viewed from the perspective of organizational sociology: resistance to technical change must be acknowledged as a reality. Couple this resistance with aversion to uncertainty, which in its turn is perceived to threaten the balance of power within an organization and between that organization and the world around it.

The desire to reduce uncertainty appears in several areas and can be satisfied in various ways. The uncertainty that new technology entails is not only in respect to profitability. New technology calls for new standards of competence, an altered organizational structure, and new patterns of working together with other firms. More often than not such changes are regarded as threats. The expression "dynamic conservatism" has been coined to describe both how conservative organizations are and how inventive and dynamic they can be when it comes to defending their established positions and roles.

Many current technical systems within the energy sector are highly capital-intensive. A long time period must often elapse from the go-ahead to invest until a plant comes on stream. To cope with the uncertainties that often exist in these cases, a common practice is to enter into long-term contracts of various kinds. As a general rule, the greater the uncertainty the longer the contract. Developments in the field of the nuclear fuel cycle are typical: whenever there is growing uncertainty about nuclear power's expansion rate, demands for long-term bindings are tightened up in the uranium mining stage, the enrichment stage, and the reprocessing stage. Another component of the quest to reduce uncertainty in capital investment projects with long service lives is to design the tariff-rate structure so that economic demand keeps increasing all along and the organization is guaranteed a smooth and stable expansion.

Long-term contracts and demand-stimulating rate structures can be said to provide an organization with the means to dominate and bind its environment and in that way reduce the uncertainty.

From this perspective, the fight over nuclear power and back pressure can be seen as a struggle for power between an organization, the State Power Board, which depended on a smooth and steady expansion and chose technology accordingly, and a group of distributors who saw back pressure as a way of reducing their dependence on the board.

Taking all things together, one can see the history of the State Power Board during the twentieth century as a series of steps for increasing its dominance, first over electricity production and later over the whole electricity sector.

The report which the Electricity Distribution Commission turned over in 1975 can be viewed in the same perspective. The question of whether those electric power distribution firms which are not now municipal ought to be run independently or by local authorities or the central government is very much a question of dominance. According to the Swedish Association of Local Authorities, municipalities ought to take over local distribution of electric power if they so wish, whereas the electricity producers prefer to see distribution separated from the municipalities. It would undoubtedly be easier for the producers to dominate the distributors if the latter were detached, rather than municipally owned, entities.

Questions of this type bear crucially upon the introduction of new technology. Fuel cells, wind power, diesel units for electricity generation, and waste heat affect the balance of power in the systems.

One of the most important lessons taught by the fight over nuclear power/combined power and heating is the stiff opposition to joining two distinct technical systems such as district heating and electricity. The competences, the experiences, the terms and conditions—all are unlike.

To tap waste heat emanating from factories for, say, district heating, is also to link together two separate activities. Such linkages appear to increase uncertainty for both systems; from this it may be surmised that it will take tough measures to make the connections. In the case of waste heat the principal actor is the National Board of Industry.

Today's energy producers appear to prefer trying to dominate their environment. Capital expenditures, lead times, and planning horizons are such that trying to dominate is natural behavior.

There is another basic way to deal with uncertainty. That is to aim activity in a direction so that it can quickly adjust itself to changes and variations. This is sometimes called adaptive behavior. The choice of an organization either to dominate or to adapt accompanies the choice of technologies.

The present tendency of the American electric utilities to opt for power stations with relatively short construction periods is an attempt to increase adaptivity.

To sum up, a coal and/or breeder solution would for all practical purposes be most likely to sharpen the demands on the energy producer to dominate his environment and guarantee a stable market. A renewable-sources solution will exacerbate the uncertainty of today's energy producers and diminish their chances of dominating.

It follows that the renewable solution must be backed up by powerful interests, by an entrepreneur. It can be boldly asserted that it is going to be pretty rough fitting a renewable-sources solution into today's systems. This holds in particular for those technologies which link activities that until now have been so independent of each other or those which in some other radical fashion alter the prerequisites for an activity. Hence wind power, heat pumps, and fuel cells may be discussed from this perspective, among others. It is still too early to say anything about what countermoves this might provoke from the energy supply system which now dominates.

A Few Words About the Interorganizational System of Rules

Let's return to the example showing the growth of the electricity sector and summarize it in a number of points:

— There is an interdependence between technical design and organizational division of responsibilities.
— By technical system we mean the whole chain from for instance falling water to appliances used by the end consumer.

— By organizational division of responsibilities we mean not only
how the individual organizations are built up but also—and
above all—what their mutual responsibility relationships look
like. By way of example we can take the division of responsibilities between the State Power Board and the individual
electricity producers, where the Board is both competitor and
sole franchiser of the trunk grid necessary for all parties. This
interorganizational system of rules also contains rules and
contracts for financing, rate-setting, and technical standards.
— A new technology is judged according to how well it fits into
the existing structure. That holds both for profitability and
for the social structure with professional groups who always
surround a given technology.
— Economic profitability is in turn determined by a system of
rules which are adapted to the existing technology.
— The interorganizational system of rules thus functions as a
filter in the introduction of new technology.

It follows that understanding how this filter works is an important
part of analyzing whether new technologies can be introduced in
the first place.

So far the role played by Parliament and Cabinet when it comes
to introducing new technology has consisted mainly of adjusting
the existing system of rules to the demands of a technology promoted from the outside.

As we discussed earier, the transition from coal to oil did not
require any changes in the administrative filter, whereas the
transition from coal-based to hydropower-based electricity generation required very big changes in the rule system. Similarly,
the introduction of nuclear power has necessitated some intensive
legislative labors, at the same time that the introduction of combined power and heating plants took place in all essentials within
the framework of the existing interorganizational system of rules.

If Parliament and Cabinet are going to assume a broader
responsibility for technical change they must also get a better
handle on the existing system of rules.

We shall therefore make an attempt to reify what we mean by the interorganizational system of rules. To begin with, we shall distinguish between function and organization. To illustrate, the following functions are of importance for the energy sector:

— to control raw materials such as uranium, falling water, and crude oil;
— to convert these into energy via nuclear power plants, hydropower plants, and refineries;
— to transport energy via trunk grids, pipelines, and other means;
— to distribute energy retail via electricity distribution societies, filling stations, and other outlets;
— to manufacture appliances and equipment for consumers of energy;
— to steer/monitor/support different aspects of the system such as safety, price level and the working environment;
— to pursue research and development and other activities on behalf of the system.

One and the same organization may now perform several functions. The Swedish State Power Board owns, produces, controls, and transports within the electricity system. The State Power Board is beginning to develop equipment for consumers (heat pumps), participate financially in gas companies, oil companies, and so forth. The oil companies are vertically integrated all the way from oil fields to gasoline pumps and have also begun to engage in consumption (heating service).

Certain supporting or regulating functions are performed by organizations which operate exclusively in the energy sphere, such as the Central Operating Management, the Swedish Nuclear Inspectorate, industrywide trade associations, and the like. Other supporting functions are handled by organizations which also have many other duties; examples are the National Price and Cartel Office, the National Board of Occupational Safety and Health, the National Environment Protection Board, the National Housing Board, the National Board of Urban Planning, and the commercial banks.

Together all these organizations shore up a system of rules for division of responsibilities which somehow depict the technical system. Thus the principles for write-offs or depreciation, the possibility of making allocations to reserves, the terms of loans, and so forth determine financing terms and as such have great importance for the setting of tariff rates. These rules are only partly specific to the energy area (e.g. the legislation concerning corporations and the Municipal Administration Act) and only partly formulated as laws. Nor are principles governing the formation of contracts between power producers and transporters (i.e., the State Power Board) regulated by law. Moreover, the State Power Board is the only state-owned trading agency in Sweden that is entitled to set its own rates. Rules on voltage, number of cycles, and variations in these are necessary to coordinate the production of appliances and energy with operation of the system. Such rules are vital to the system and are administered via agreements reached within the trade associations. As such they fall wholly outside the legislative scope. Similarly, agreements between owners of combined power and heating plants (i.e., the municipalities) and the State Power Board on the terms governing purchases of stand-by power in case the plant stands idle are not regulated in detail by law. Nonetheless such rules may have crucial bearing upon the profitability of a combined power and heating plant. Finally, such things as the provisions of legislation on health and safety at work are playing an increasingly important role in various branches of economic activity. One need only think of the asbestos problems in combined power and heating plants or the plutonium discussion in connection with the nuclear fuel cycle.

The point we want to make with all these examples is that the interorganizational system of rules is a complicated filter, whereas the rules embodied in law are no more than the top of an administrative iceberg. A very large part of the filter has been built up by the concerned organizations themselves—within the framework of general laws such as the Companies Act.

Will the renewable energy sources be able to pass through

this filter? We do not know that yet; we need a better grasp of the specific demands they impose. Even so, a few examples can give a foretaste of the problems:

Solar collectors for heating purposes will require, among other things, an adjusting amendment to the housing loan ordinance. If government authorities are especially eager to stimulate such technology, special measures such as incentive allowances may be necessary.

Wind power for the generation of electricity is perhaps attractive chiefly to small electricity producers and distributors, who can use wind power to make themselves partly independent of the larger producers. But wind power plants will call for adjustment of the legislation on building and planning (the appearance of sites, rules on awards of damages for land trespassing, safety regulations for construction projects, and so forth). Moreover, the setting of tariff rates for standby power must be adjusted and, if wind power comes into widespread use, the whole system that accounts for Swedish energy system balances will be changed. This will presumably affect the rate setting for plants not based on wind power also.

Fuel cells, say for the generation of electricity, are by no means unreasonable propositions in the long run. If they can be used on the household or neighborhood level, tremendous changes would be wrought in the stipulations for electric power supply. The economics of fuel cells would then depend on whether they qualify for government funding (the housing loan ordinance), whether the heat losses in them can be tapped for space heating (which in its turn affects the division of responsibilities between landlord and tenant), whether there exist a subsidiary market for the fuel in question, and so forth. Also affected will be the fire protection rules, the Product Control Act, and building and planning legislation.

It must be emphasized accordingly that the real obstacle cannot be imputed for sure to those rules that are construed *at this moment* to be primarily motivated by energy policy. Perhaps the roadblocks are thrown up by stipulations of quite another kind, such as those governing the relationships of tenant, housing administrator, housebuilder, and the capital market.

So the concept "filter" must not be interpreted as the sum total of those rules about which it is explicitly stated that they are energy-policy motivated and in one way or another monitored by organizations with a legitimate mission within the energy sector. The verdict may be decided just as well by rules which are based on totally different frames of reference, such as occupational safety and the like—rules which perhaps ought to be changed.

On the Role of Parliament and Cabinet

A review of the history of energy policy during the twentieth century shows that government authorities seldom take direct stands for or against specific technical systems or technical solutions. The only conspicuous exceptions to this picture were the decisions to electrify the railways, the decisions of principle to electrify rural areas and farms, and—naturally—the nuclear power decisions of the 1970s.

It may be assumed that summit-level decision-making capacity is such that it is only by way of exception that one can go straightaway into the development of new technical systems. (The formal process leading from initiatives to parliamentary decisions and their implementation via investigation by committees, governmental bills, and parliamentary debate is of itself a limiting factor.) Interventions of this kind also seem to be rare in other areas, being restricted to certain key sectors such as the national defense, education, and broadcasting.

It may also be assumed that Parliament and Cabinet seldom or never find themselves in situations where a "decision point" is imposed from the outside. So in practice they have never been confronted with a choice between two equivalent systems. If anything the choice has stood between system "x" and chaos, destitution, and unemployment.

Should this be taken to mean that government authorities are powerless in the face of technological advance; that they will be forced all along to take stands on excruciating alternatives (within energy policy) whenever different supply crises come to the fore?

In our society we are agreed that "all power emanates from the people" and that this power is exercised by Parliament and Cabinet in compliance with certain formal rules. But it does not follow from this that government authorities take a stand on every single issue. Parliament and Cabinet "steer" the society and social development not by intervening directly in every social and economic decision-making situation but by laying down rules on how different actors may behave towards one another or toward the environment. In other words, government authorities do not choose technical systems directly; instead they choose an organization which in turn creates the concrete reality according to its lights.

The majority of such decisions on ground rules in society—on social organization, that is—are strategic. It is not always easy to isolate the effects on particular social areas. Knowledge of the consequences of decisions is often imperfect. That which seemed to be a perfect and functional division of labor (as between energy producers and energy consumers) in one situation may in another situation—and much later on—evoke the very crisis and the defective freedom of action that we want to avoid.

Here again we can make use of the filter concept. The role of Parliament and Cabinet is to create a filter which lets through only the desirable technical solutions and no others. The difficulties should not be underestimated. For various reasons the rule-making machinery of social organization will be an almost immutable part of the real world. The Norwegian legal scholar, Vilhelm Aubert, makes this observation:

There are many obstacles to a rapid and effective self-regulation and self-correction in the production of legal rules. The lawmaking apparatus bears great resemblances to a large assembly of machinery, a body of real capital to which massive investments are tied down. Even if there are political grounds for extensive reforms, there is an immense inertia in the amount of work that is put into the existing set of rules.

Just as the physical structure of real properties and communities thwart many reforms in human coexistence patterns, so does many a reform plan run smack into the socio-organizational "concrete wall" that the legal system represents.

Conditions are complicated even more by the modern tendency to enact so-called framework laws. This means that governmental intentions are given a relatively general locution in the primary legislation, while the courts and, more often, the administrative agencies are mandated to put flesh on the statutory bones. This is a flexible method from many vantages because the legislative particulars can be rather easily adapted to technological development or to other more superficial changes in society. Most likely, too, it is necessary in a modern society. But at the same time it implies that couplings to organizational and other vested interests are made, which result in the inertia in the change process becoming even harder to handle.

We therefore conclude that by far the greater part of technical change steered by Parliament and Cabinet, and hence by the political process, travels an indirect route. Other than in exceptional cases, we cannot have thoroughgoing debates and political decisions on the shaping of technology. Direct steerage demands too much attention and time from hard-pressed decision makers.

So the most important type of influence brought to bear on future technical change is the indirect one—via the system of rules and roles which government authorities define through legislation, organizational structuring, and so forth.

The consequences for freedom of action in energy policy are fairly obvious. Today's organizational design finds it easy to handle large-scale production such as hydropower, nuclear power, and coal-based power. Handling the renewable energy sources proves much tougher. If these sources are going to stand a chance of being regarded as a real alternative, there must be a back-up organizational structure, an array of entrepreneurs, who will make it *their* interest to operate the renewable energy sources. Hence the most important contribution that Parliament and Cabinet can render to an energy policy dedicated to greater freedom of action is to create opportunities for such an organizational structure. This in turn means that the present structure must adapt or be forced to adapt itself accordingly.

Supporting Activities Required for the Various Solutions

Earlier in this chapter ("Organizations and Uncertainty") we pointed out that different energy technologies vary in the demands they impose on supporting activities such as the capital market, construction projects, the division of responsibilities between public and private bodies, central and local bodies, and so forth.

Let us therefore set up some hypotheses as to which demands the various solutions put on surrounding activities. Although table 11 is to be seen as an intellectual experiment, it does indicate that the solutions will probably bring vastly different structural consequences.

Such a table can be elaborated of course. But to our minds it definitely suggests that it won't be all that easy to have both solutions at the same time: there is a tendency to end up either on one track or the other.

It should be emphasized that one cannot call the one alternative more decentralized than the other. If anything, one must discuss the individual with reference to his or her different roles— as consumer, as politically active person, and as employee. And then it would seem as though, say, a coal and/or breeder solution makes for an energy supply which gives the individual as consumer great freedom of choice—after all, electricity is extremely practical and flexible—but in contrast less freedom of choice as a political person.

Decisions on siting nuclear power plants, on the components of the fuel cycle, on coaling ports and coal hauls, and on facilities

TABLE 11
EXAMPLES OF STRUCTURAL CONSEQUENCES OF DIFFERENT
ENERGY TECHNOLOGY SOLUTIONS

	Coal and/or breeders	Renewable sources
Capital market	Huge capital amounts to be shared out among a small number (only one?) of recipients.	Huge capital amounts shall be shared out among a great many recipients (households, property owners, municipalities, firms).
Civil engineering	A small number of big building sites. Ambulating specialists.	A great many smaller building sites, with ample provision for job rotation.
Division of responsibilities (central/local)	Municipal veto right will probably have to be abolished for the energy sector's components (cf. mining of uranium). Strengthens central vis-à-vis local bodies.	Certain rights and liberties now enjoyed by households will probably have to be transferred to municipal bodies. Strengthens local bodies vis-à-vis households and other units.
Division of responsibilities (public/private)	Interwoven interests: central administration/ big firms.	Interwoven interests: municipal bodies, residential areas, local workplaces.
Professional groups	Great need for highly qualified specialists with little alternate value. Technocratic elite.	Great need for broadly educated persons able to adapt local energy sources to local conditions.
Central electricity system	Dominates its environment.	Dominated by its environment. Functions mainly as standby and backup system.

for the production of gas or synthetic fuels must be fitted into a national plan and can hardly be permitted to be overthrown by local opinions. So, seen from this viewpoint the individual's freedom of choice is narrowed.

In the renewable alternative the individual as consumer would appear to have less freedom of choice. Energy will probably be in shorter supply, and he will probably be forced to accept having to adapt to a local energy supply system built up around local determinants. The demand for fair nationwide share-outs of scarce resources will be strongly voiced, and it is not all sure that the individual as political being will perceive himself to be any less "centrally regimented."

Put differently: we do not think there is any simple connection between large-scale/small-scale technology and the degree of centralization/decentralization.

Organization Design for Freedom of Action: Is There One?

Let us summarize the thoughts advanced in this chapter. Our object is to provoke a discussion of how the energy supply can be organized to give the renewable energy sources a chance to become more than a disembodied technological wraith. As a matter of course such a discussion will be loose and groping, but we still think it feasible to single out a number of questions that are worth asking as well as subjects deserving further study.

We have two initial premises:

— technical and organizational designs are interdependent;
— revolutionary technical change increases uncertainty and is perceived as a threat by those organizations with vested interests in existing technology.

The evidence indicates that the coal and/or breeder solution makes a better fit with today's organizational structure than the renewable energy sources do. It is therefore reasonable to imagine that a vigorous commitment to energy conservation and renewable energy sources will be perceived as a threat by those organizations which are primarily oriented to today's energy production systems (for example nuclear power, oil).

A third premise (well anchored in the literature on organization) states:

— every organization strives to avoid uncertainty and to safeguard its own existence. To expand at just the right rate is one means of reducing uncertainty.

After all, introducing renewable energy sources implies that the present organizations will have less room to expand inside their customary operational domains. Even a vigorously pursued policy of energy conservation has the same consequence. Most of the measures which are discussed—additional insulation, energy taxes, and so forth—act to cut back the room into which existing organizations can expand but do not lessen their expansion needs. How can the expansion needs of the present energy sector be reduced?

It must be emphasized that these expansion needs are not anything illegitimate or shameful. On the contrary, they express a dynamic force, an inventiveness—call it what you will—that should not be suffocated but guided in the right direction. If innovative talent cannot be given room for free play in one direction, it should be encouraged to thrive in another direction. As noted, we attach great weight to the interorganizational division of responsibilities when it comes to understanding why, for instance, the electricity producers do as they do. Hence the fundamental question is this: can Parliament and Cabinet change the terms governing today's energy supply systems so as to encourage renewable energy sources and restraint in energy usage?

The basic assumption should be that it is not energy in general but specific kinds of energy that we want to husband or manage economically. This is true of oil, coal, nuclear power, and hydro-power. However, there are no reasons (today) to save on solar energy, wind energy, and similar renewable sources.

Therefore we ask: can the terms and conditions under which the suppliers of energy produced by means of fossil fuels, nuclear power, and hydropower be changed so as to make these persons feel not only an interest in and responsibility for the expansion of nuclear power or fossil-fired power plants but also for measures which can reduce the future need for these particular energy types?

Steps in this direction have been taken in the United States. A number of American public utilities have applied for permission to invest their capital in energy-saving measures among consumers as a complement/alternative to spending these same funds on the production of more energy.

The Swedish oil companies have partly embarked on this road. Today they are competing not only with oil sales but also with heating service, that is, maintenance and care of oil furnaces. In so doing, they have taken a first (small) step toward offering energy-saving measures. One may ask whether the companies may also be led into offering a more complete range of energy-saving measures, such as mapping out weak points in building structures, improved insulation, and switching over to triple-pane windows.

The oil companies are motivated to offer heating service on sheer commercial grounds. They compete with one another and with electric heating in this way. But can the conditions of private enterprise be changed so as to make it commercially attractive to enlarge services of this kind? Can the electricity producers be persuaded to move in the same direction?

A first step is to make the analyses of alternatives to increased electric power generation mandatory. According to NEPA (the American counterpart to our Environment Protection Act) American electricity producers may not be licensed to expand production unless they have submitted an environmental impact report. This document must not only state what environmental consequences the power plant project in question will have but also demonstrate that there is no more effective way of achieving the same result, as by investing equivalent capital in energy-saving measures. A draft law of similar purport is now being discussed in Switzerland.

But it is doubtful whether more information is enough. Be that as it may, we can note that the American electricity producers and the Swedish oil companies do have direct contact with consumers. It then becomes conceivable to balance measures to produce energy against measures to save it. However, this observation does not hold for the Swedish system of electricity supply, where a distributor sometimes comes in between producer and consumer. Would it then be possible even here to get producers and distributors interested in saving energy? In that case the distribution of responsibilities among consumers, distributors, and producers will have to be changed root and branch.

The consumer must be stimulated to study energy saving as a worthwhile alternative. That stimulus can come from the setting of tariff rates, the terms of delivery, and other measures. The distributor must then be made to feel that he will not be automatically duty-bound to deliver constantly increasing amounts of energy to consumers. Perhaps that can be brought about in two ways: through changes in the terms of delivery vis-à-vis consumers and through changes in those terms which the distributor has vis-à-vis producers.

The distributors will be under pressure to help the consumers save electricity if the producers in their turn (are forced to) impose demands on the distributors. The demands on producers and distributors can be incorporated when applications are filed for licenses to expand distribution grids and energy production. But they can also be incorporated at the point of transaction between producers and distributors.

We do not know whether it is possible to impose demands on energy producers and distributors that will make them see it as in their own interests to expand an organization dedicated to saving energy. In our opinion, however, this matter should be investigated. Perhaps one way of making progress may be to change the organization of energy supply so as to eliminate the coupling between producer and distributor and turn it into an instrument for energy conservation.

In the case of electricity this coupling is represented by the trunk grid. The one who controls that grid can impose terms both on producers and distributors. For the electricity sector this would mean putting the trunk grid, and perhaps the regional grid too, in the charge of a specially designated governing authority. In that case, for reasons that will be developed below, distribution should also be organizationally separated from production. One consequence will then be that bulk consumers (e.g., factories) do not directly negotiate with the producer but with those who control the trunk grid. As a result the trunk grid (i.e., the electricity transport system) would primarily be seen as an instrument for pursuing a policy of balancing electricity supply and demand and not as a system for transporting energy at minimum cost.

Now how do things look for the other important energy types? Large parts of the trunk grid's counterpart in the oil sector lie outside Sweden, but it is conceivable that the refineries comprise a similarly critical point that can be used for strategic control of (oil) economizing measures.

One question that must be studied more closely is how tariff rates, and along with them such matters as financing terms, should be designed so as to stimulate conservation rather than increased production. As we have seen earlier, expanding production at just the right rate comes with a built-in advantage due to rigidities, indivisibilities, and a high proportion of capital costs. Progressive tariff rates could be designed so as specifically to seek to stimulate conservation: the more the consumer disposes of, the more he would be made to pay for the next kWh. But in that case the financial situation for producers and distributors would have to be analyzed. One can entertain the hypothesis that such a rate structure would so increase the uncertainty about future usage as to motivate the energy producers to increase their adaptability and avoid rigid and indivisible systems. Although energy-saving measures, renewable energy sources, and so forth are admittedly capital-intensive, they do not at all have the same drawbacks in the form of indivisibilities and long lead times associated with large-scale energy production.

Next, how to go about creating an organizational base for renewable energy sources. There are two problems here. First, how shall entrepreneurs be stimulated to tackle different renewable energy sources? Second, how can institutions be created which can integrate renewable energy sources, energy-saving measures, and energy from today's energy producers with a system of energy management plans? This integration would go across the board: locally, regionally, and nationally.

Now how does one stimulate entrepreneurs to take up the cudgel for different renewable energy sources? They shall play the role of devising technology and arguing for the introduction of renewable energy sources and work on those who are responsible for the system of rules so that rules which might stymie these sources are placed under debate. It will be necessary to contemplate solutions that differ from one technology to another; for present purposes we mention only a few examples of likely entrepreneurs:

Several technologies—such as solar collectors for heating and, possibly in the future, solar cells for electricity generation— depend for their profitability on various factors, not least the need for materials (glass, sheet metal, aluminum, and so on). In turn this means that part of their profitability depends on whether they have been integrated with other activities, such as housing construction. It is therefore natural to think of the building sector as carrier of some of these technologies, but also think of the organizational structure of the whole building administration. Should rental legislation be amended to encourage today's housing administrators to become entrepreneurs?

Other technologies, such as those based on biomass for fuel

production, enjoy a natural market either in combined power and heating plants run by local authorities or in pyrolysis plants. Here forestry and agriculture seem to be likely carriers, together with municipal bodies on the energy and waste side.

Certain technologies already have likely entrepreneurs. Wind power, for instance, is a conceivable alternative to the generation of electricity by distributors and small producers.

Although fuel cells per se do not have anything to do with renewable energy sources, they can play a very big role together with other technologies. Fuel cells can be used as a method of storing electricity. The big utilities today comprise one class of entrepreneur that can use fuel cells as integral parts of their systems. Inevitably, the installations involved will be large and complicated. Other likely entrepreneurs are municipal energy companies and/or the building industry or building administrators who can strive to bring out simple fuel cells which could be used perhaps at the neighborhood level. Higher operating costs of electricity generation could then be justified by taking advantage of waste heat for space heating.

Suffice it to say that the current scene does not lack opportunities for finding entrepreneurs to back renewable technology. But our observation comes with a caveat: these entrepreneurs do not coincide with today's energy producers, nor do they now have any competence for handling these matters (with some exception made for the building industry, where work on solar collectors has started up in a small way). Here again, of course, it is true that the system of rules can be harnessed to stimulate entrepreneurs. Today, for instance, there are standards which lay down what kind of insulation should be installed in new houses. What would happen instead if one were to introduce standards on how much energy may be delivered from the outside (electricity, oil, district heating, and so on)? And what if the government's lending rules were to be designed accordingly?

How does one now set about strengthening the integrating role? The redistribution of roles to stimulate energy conservation, along with measures to stimulate entrepreneurs, will undoubtedly escalate conflict. It will be necessary to have some sort of integrating process to balance saving measures against measures to produce different types of energy.

The question is whether there is any possibility other than placing the responsibility for balancing energy supply and demand on the municipalities. A first step in this direction was taken with the proposals put forward in 1976 by the Commission on Municipal Energy Planning. But then it will probably be necessary to distinguish between two functions: husbanding energy and producing energy. After all, many municipalities are producers of electricity and district heating.

Up till now the distribution process has been seen exclusively as an instrument for finding (and increasing) sales for the output. If municipalities are to be vested with a husbanding responsibility, distribution will have to been seen as one of the husbanding stages, and as such, moreover, as an instrument for holding back those interests that want to increase production—irrespective of whether the producer is owned by central government, local authorities, or private investors.

If local authorities are to be vested with responsibility for husbanding energy, distribution will have to be managed at municipal level, that is, the basic units of local government as opposed to the tier represented by the county councils (at least for that form of energy which is bound to power lines).

Today there is a desire on the part of electricity producers to keep the distribution of electric power separated from other activities—preferably neither a state-run nor a municipally-run operation; however, if distribution is municipally run, then integrated as little as possible with the municipality's other activities. One of their compelling reasons is to make sure that electricity distributors do not charge higher rates than their costs warrant. Such an attitude is quite understandable since higher rates dampen effective demand for the producers' electricity. As we see it, that is the wrong way to go. The distributors of energy should not be divorced from other activities but intentionally integrated with them.

What should such a municipal husbanding organization look like? It should be kept apart from the municipal producer interests. But other than that it should encompass other scarce resources as well, such as waste and water.

Such integration on the local level must have some sort of counterpart on the national level. Somebody must be responsible for seeing to it that the relations of distributors with consumers and producers (whether oil or electricity is involved) actually work and provide impetus to energy conservation. This responsibility belongs to governmental and private producer interests as well as to those specialized organizations that have to monitor other areas than energy husbanding, such as the National Environment Protection Board, the National Housing Board, the National Board of Industry, and the National Board of Urban Planning. Is it possible to have one government agency which looks after energy husbanding and nothing else? The answer is not immediately apparent.

Summing up, we ask ourselves these questions before continuing with our work:

— Can the division of responsibilities among consumers, distributors and producers be changed so as to give the producers an added incentive to help the consumers save energy?
— Would it not be appropriate on the electricity side to devise a special intermediary between production and consumption through which Parliament and Cabinet could exercise strategic control and stimulate conservation?
— Can ways be found to stimulate entrepreneurs on behalf of the renewable energy sources?
— Is it feasible to create special organizations to integrate the different components of the energy husbanding program?

There is no doubt that such changes in the energy system will increase the uncertainties and the level of conflicts—and will be resisted by today's producer interests. But the question remains whether there is any other way of holding the door open to a renewable alternative in the future.

8
Nuclear Power in Sweden's Energy Future: Commitments and Alternatives

Introduction

SWEDEN WAS ONE of the first countries apart from those possessing nuclear weapons to develop a large nuclear power program. This was in many ways a natural outcome, since Sweden has no fossil fuels but does have considerable amounts of (admittedly low-grade) uranium and high technological competence. Swedish industry also developed an LWR design of its own without any licenses from other countries. At the beginning of the 1970s a large nuclear power program was judged necessary, but by the mid-seventies the industry was plunged into political controversy.

This chapter traces the development of the nuclear power program as part of Swedish energy policy and attempts to assess the political situation. A solar alternative to nuclear energy is described, together with an an analysis of the inertia that favors a continued nuclear program.

Establishing Nuclear Power: Pushing and Pulling

Dependence on imported energy has been a major issue in the Swedish debate on energy policy since the beginning of the century, when indigenous wood was replaced by imported coal. Oil imports expanded rapidly after the Second World War and now account for 70 percent of Sweden's energy balance. Thus low cost of fuel has been valued consistently more than independence, and the net effect has been a dramatic increase in imports.

Nuclear power was conceived of as the only indigenous source that would offer independence, be economical, and at the same time establish Sweden on the technological forefront.

A Swedish base of research on nuclear power already had been established by 1946, both for military (production of and protection against nuclear weapons) and civilian reasons.

In 1956 a royal commission published a study in which nuclear power based on Swedish uranium was seen as one major way to come to grips with a rapidly rising dependence on imported oil. The study proposed nuclear energy for supply of district heating and for electricity. Projects for development of heavy-water reactors based on natural Swedish uranium were launched with several goals in mind. One was energy, another was industrial policy, and a third was military. During the 1950s the issue of nuclear energy was interconnected with the issue of Swedish nuclear weapons. Swedish nuclear arms would have been based on plutonium, and research aimed at power-producing (and thus plutonium-producing) uranium-fuelled reactors could thus be attributed to both civilian and military reasons. In order to avoid a serious split over weapons within the ruling party then-Prime Minister Tage Erlander pushed the Swedish civilian nuclear energy program as the only way of postponing a decision on nuclear weapons. This was the first in a series of pushes.

The end of the 1950s marked another important change. Environmental opposition toward expansion of hydropower in the North of Sweden increased, and nuclear power became one of the options for future electricity production. This opposition increased during the 1960s and constituted the second big push for nuclear power.

The earliest nuclear proposals were for heat-producing reactors (based on natural uranium and heavy water) to be connected to district heating networks. These were to use indigenous fuel rather than imported fuels such as coal and oil. The utilities, for various reasons, became increasingly skeptical about this reactor strategy, and gradually the heat-producing schemes gave way to electricity-producing reactors. A full-scale project for an electricity-producing HWR failed and was officially scrapped in 1970. By that time the private Swedish utilities had long since opted for LWRs, and a Swedish industrial base was organized (through joint ventures between the state and different private firms: ASEA-ATOM, UDDCOMB). Sweden thus became one of the few countries in the world with a reactor industry of its own and the only one outside the centrally planned economies to have developed it without a U.S. license.

During the 1960s nuclear power gradually became the accepted successor to hydropower for electricity production, and the State Power Board gradually became the entrepreneur of nuclear power in Sweden. The main alternative to electricity production during these years was electricity produced as a byproduct through back-pressure, fossil-fuelled plants. District heating expanded rapidly during the 1950s and the 1960s in Sweden and created possibilities for combined generation of heat and electricity. This development, which was favored by those cities in charge of district heating and electricity distribution, naturally threatened the market for electricity produced by nuclear power and was vigorously opposed by the power producers. Among the weapons used were rate schemes so designed as to make combined generation unprofitable.

The blocking of combined heat and power was the third big push for nuclear power, and it was followed by the fourth—which was a "pull" rather than a "push"—when the electric utilities managed to convince the construction industry that if the latter would introduce electric space-heating the former would guarantee long-term contracts of low-cost electricity. Thus a whole new market for electricity was opened up.

In 1972 the utilities forecasted a demand for electricity of 250 TWh by 1985 and possibly 400 TWh by the year 2000, nearly all supplied by nuclear. The utilities called for twenty-four reactors by 1990. Fast breeder reactors (FBRs) were regarded as the next step, and plans were made for the complete fuel cycle.

By 1973 eleven reactors, with a total generating capacity of 8,400 MW, had been licensed by the government for construction at four different sites. Nuclear energy was safely established.

Then the roof fell in.

Swedish Energy Policy in the 1970s: From Consent to Dissent

Up to 1973 all major decisions on nuclear power in the Swedish Parliament had been taken by large majorities. The debates that did take place were over different technical aspects, such as the relative merits of LWR over HWR, together with the interconnected issue of the role of the state versus private enterprise in what was regarded as a future growth industry. Nuclear power as such was never questioned; it was seen as the only way to avoid exploitation of the remaining hydropower potential in northern Sweden.

The decision-making process (under the Act of nuclear energy) allocated to the government the ultimate right of licensing reactors. The Parliament was only involved if the financing ran over the budget, that is, where the State Power Board was the owner. Reactors built by private utilities were thus never placed on the agenda of Parliament. Moreover, Swedish law does not allow outside intervention in licensing decisions on safety grounds made by the regulatory bodies.

Thus, there did not exist any national plan on the role of nuclear power in Sweden in 1973. Plans were formulated by the electric utilities and coordinated by the Central Dispatching Board, which is an organization fostering cooperation among the major Swedish electricity producers.

In sum, nuclear power was handled by government and Parliament much in the same way as energy policy in general was handled. Once the major legal barriers are removed and an industry is established, that industry is left pretty much on its own. Government intervention in the energy field generally has been minor in Sweden, compared with intervention in most other countries.

The first cracks in the roof above the nuclear program came in 1973 when questions were asked in Parliament over reactor safety and waste management. The results of this debate were twofold. First came the beginning of a split between the political parties over nuclear power, with the main (then) opposition party, the Center Party, gradually taking a stand against nuclear power. Second, Parliament declared that no new reactors should be licensed until more information was available on reactor safety and on waste handling. The commissions dealing with these matters were scheduled to have completed their work by 1974. Parliament thus requested a national plan for nuclear power and also, in effect, took over from the government ultimate responsibility for nuclear power.

By this time nuclear power had been withdrawn from its "noncontroversial" niche, placed squarely on the political agenda, and attracted mounting interest in different quarters.

A political consequence of the oil embargo and rise in oil prices in 1973 was that the decision on nuclear power had to be broadened into a decision on energy policy in general.

A debate of unparalleled intensity ensued during the fall of 1974. Among the topics not only were nuclear power but also other supply alternatives, conservation possibilities, energy forecasts, the relationships between energy and real income, employment, and environmental issues. To some extent the debate became one about industrial society as such.

The government presented a bill on energy policy which was passed by Parliament in May 1975. Its main thrust was to ensure the supply of energy until 1985 while preserving as many options as possible for the future. The major points were:

— A target to reduce growth in annual energy demand from an historical rate of over 4 percent to no more than 2 percent until 1985 and a "serious inquiry" into the possibilities of achieving zero energy growth from 1990 onwards.

— This was to be done through conservation measures primarily within industry and space heating, stimulated by the price increase in imported oil and helped by government subsidies and cheap loans.

— The nuclear program was increased from eleven reactors to thirteen, to be completed by 1985. (five reactors were already operating.

— A new major review of energy policy was scheduled to take place in 1978.

By this time nuclear power was clearly a top item of political debate. Of four opposition parties, two nonsocialist parties backed the Social Democratic government in principle. One, the Center Party, the largest opposition party, would not accept any nuclear reactors in addition to the five already operating and called for more conservation. The fourth opposition party, the Communists, also rejected nuclear power and called for a referendum.

Several important decisions were postponed by the government, and the momentum of the nuclear program was thus slowed. No new sites for reactors were proposed, the questions of waste handling and reprocessing were also postponed together with the more and more sensitive question of mining Sweden's considerable uranium deposits.

Thus by 1975 energy policy had become a highly political issue, which it had never actually been since the introduction of hydropower at the beginning of the century. The Social Democratic government was voted out of office in 1976, partially because of its nuclear program. The new government, the first nonsocialist government in forty-four years, was split apart over nuclear energy, with one party opposed and the other two in favor. The opposing party, the Center Party, was elected on a promise to phase out nuclear energy by 1985. Apart from the five reactors operating in 1976 seven were under various stages of construction.

The new government appointed a parliamentary energy commission mandated to make a major review of energy policy options in time for the decision that was scheduled for the fall of 1978.

For the time period ending in 1990 four alternatives were studied, ranging from nuclear phaseout by 1985 to continued nuclear expansion beyond the previously agreed upon thirteen-reactor program (see "Long-term supply alternatives" below). The study was published in April 1978.

A majority of the commission, consisting of the major opposition party (the Social Democrats) and two of the government parties, supported the 1975 nuclear program, while the majority, consisting among others of the third government party, called for a gradual phase out of nuclear power by 1990.

The new government also had to make a series of compromises over the reactor program. The Nuclear Energy Law was amended in late 1976, requiring that reactor licenses should be granted by the government only after each licensee had come up with an acceptable scheme for waste management. The law was made partially retroactive, applicable to all reactors under construction but not to those already operating. This law was seen by the pronuclear parties as a way to force the utilities to put forward a scheme for waste disposal, and the parties had no serious doubts that the government would be able to accept the proposal rather soon and thus grant the licenses. The antinuclear party, however, saw the law and its safety conditions as an unsurmountable barrier to the further expansion of nuclear energy. The precise conditions under which the proposals should be accepted or rejected were never spelled out in the law.

The utilities submitted their proposal in late 1977, and this was subject to an extensive technical review. After lengthy negotiations the government reached agreement on how to handle the proposal—but resigned in October 1978 over the role of nuclear power in general and the role of the Swedish nuclear industry in particular.

The antinuclear party was prepared to accept the fueling of reactors seven to ten provided a commitment was made not to go beyond this program. This would have killed the reactor industry, and the other two parties were not prepared to go along at that time. The agreement over fueling meant that the Swedish NRC was in effect given the mandate to issue a license once it was proven that there does exist a suitable place for ultimate waste disposal. After test drillings had taken place at two sites, and after some controversy over the geological evidence put forward, the Swedish NRC recommended drilling in March 1979.

A new government was formed by the Liberal Party, with the backing of 39 seats out of 349 in Parliament. The government published a bill on energy policy in early March 1979. This called for twelve reactors to be operating in 1990. No more nuclear power plants were to be installed, according to this bill. The Three-Mile Island accident, in late March 1979, triggered a decision to hold a referendum on nuclear energy in March 1980. Thus the parts of the bill which deal with nuclear energy have been deferred until the outcome of the referendum is clear. In the September 1979 election, the non-Socialist parties gained a majority of one seat (out of 349) and have formed a new coalition government.

The biggest short-term problem seems to be the fate of the Swedish reactor industry. This was originally designed for a more rapidly increasing demand for electricity and a much larger nuclear program than that which is needed today even under optimistic forecasts of energy demand. The present nuclear program, together with some more hydropower, combined generation plants, electricity conservation, and, possibly, wind power, could supply Sweden with electricity until the end of the century. Such a program, however, would not sustain the Swedish reactor industry.

Thus the energy policy of the new government—or of any government—will have to face two issues. The first is the fate of the Swedish reactor industry, and the second is the long-term direction of the Swedish energy supply system. We shall return to the conflict between the two after the second issue has been dealt with.

Long-term Supply Alternatives

When nuclear energy is as controversial as it is the controversy tends to spread to associated issues. One concerns demand forecasts in general.

Figure 13 shows various energy-demand forecasts made since 1972.

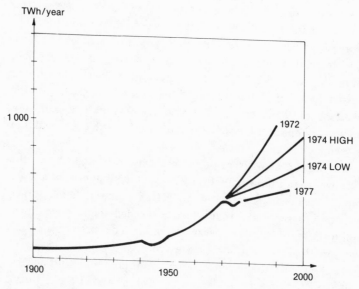

Fig. 13. Energy demand forecasts since 1972.

Reductions depend partly on assumptions of reduced economic growth. Later forecasts also include the impact of conservation and higher prices. The impact of price elasticity is controversial. So is the question of the extent to which consumption patterns (i.e., lifestyles) should be seen as an acceptable way of influencing long-term energy demand. Another controversy centers on the role conservation can play, the speed with which it could be implemented, and the degree of invention that is acceptable in order to ensure that implementation. A third area of controversy concerns alternatives to nuclear power, in particular oil and solar energy. There is a tendency among opponents of nuclear power to be optimistic about global oil supply *and* the technological development of solar energy, and there is a corresponding but reversed tendency among the proponents of nuclear to be pessimistic.

In order to clarify the issues the energy commission studied four alternative patterns for Swedish midterm energy policy in general and for nuclear energy in particular. All were based on the 1977 demand forecast shown in figure 13.

The time frame is from the present until 1990, but the four alternatives studied are seen as having different long-term implications (see table 12; one of the alternatives has a subcase).

The alternatives have been evaluated in terms of their effects on environment, economy, and capital requirements. Impacts during the 1980s differ markedly, and alternative A in particular imposes severe strains on the economy. Averaged out over a twenty-one-year period, even the two extreme alternatives (A and D) differ by not more than 10 percent, however. Alternative C^1 is the most favorable from an economic point of view. Uncertainties are obviously great, but one conclusion is rather firm: expansion of nuclear power beyond the present program is not the most efficient way of reducing oil imports. There is no simple exchange relation between oil and nuclear energy.

A, B, and D can be seen as first steps on different, but rather

TABLE 12
ALTERNATIVES TO NUCLEAR POWER

	Medium-term perspective	Major substitutes for oil and nuclear (cases A and B)	Percent reduction in oil import in 1990 relative to 1977	Annual total cost 1979-2000, Sw Crs per capita	Long-term direction
A	Phase out nuclear to 1985	Conservation, gas, biomass, peat	13	4,900	Solar
B	Phase out nuclear to 1990	Conservation, gas, peat, wind	10	4,800	Solar
C	Complete 1975 nuclear program (10–13 reactors)	Conservation, gas, some peat, nuclear	20	4,500	Solar and/or nuclear
C¹		Same plus increased conservation	33	4,200	
D	Expand nuclear beyond 1975 program	Conservation, some coal, some peat, nuclear (heat and electricity)	25	4,500	Nuclear and limited amounts of solar

well-defined tracks. Only C is undefined in this respect. As noted earlier, this alternative was backed by a large political majority. The need for freedom of action was stressed.

THE SWEDISH NUCLEAR INDUSTRY

The different alternatives of the energy commission imply distinct futures for the Swedish nuclear industry. Only in alternative D (table 12) does it have a guaranteed market. This industry is not so much a single industry as a group of industries, organized around the Swedish electromechanical industry, ASEA. The nuclear subdivision, ASEA-ATOM, is owned jointly by ASEA and the Swedish state, employs roughly two thousand persons, and is mainly a design and engineering company. Some very specialized components are also manufactured by ASEA-ATOM, but all major components are subcontracted. The turbines are made by Stal-Laval, and the pressurized vessels are made by UDDCOMB, a company with up to 75 percent state ownership and up to 25 percent Combustion Engineering ownership. Stal-Laval manufactures turbines on a license from BBC (Brown-Boveri) and is explicitly forbidden to export turbines for nuclear reactors unless it is for an export order secured by ASEA-ATOM. UDDCOMB manufactures vessels also for other nuclear vendors in Europe.

The capacity of the industry is roughly 1–2 GWpa; the required ordering level for staying in the black is said to be roughly 1 GWpa; and the level required for maintaining competence is estimated by ASEA-ATOM to be one order every second or third year. The company needs another order, roughly, before the end of 1981 in order to maintain its design team.

The situation in this industry does not differ very much from that of other nuclear-reactor suppliers around the world (apart from the French supplier Framatome). The industry was established at a time when forecasts for nuclear-generated electricity were much higher, as can be seen in table 13.

TABLE 13

TWO FORECASTS OF ELECTRICITY DEMAND IN THE YEAR
1990, MADE IN 1972 AND 1977 BY THE CENTRAL OPERATING
MANAGEMENT—A JOINT ORGANIZATION OF MAJOR
SWEDISH POWER PRODUCERS (CDL).

	Electricity use 1975 TWh	1972 forecast for 1990 TWh	1977 forecast for 1990 TWh
Industry	39	110	66
Comercial	13	50	26
Households, excl space-heating	12	28	15
Households, space-heating	6	27	18
Second homes	1	4	3.5
Total incl losses	82	250	153

The 1972 forecast estimated the total installed nuclear capacity to be 25 GW by 1990 and perhaps 60 GW by the year 2000. This, of course, would have given the nuclear industry a comfortable market.

By contrast the 1977 forecast requires roughly 10 GW by the year 1990. Other studies have shown lower total electricity demand by the 1990s, partly through the effect of higher prices. It is therefore likely that increased use of cogeneration and some more hydropower, coupled with restrictive use of electric space-heating and some conservation methods, would mean that no new orders for reactors have to be placed at least during the 1980s, and possibly well into the 1990s. Beyond that the future demand for nuclear energy depends on whether solar alternatives are feasible or not. Such a development, however, would kill the Swedish nuclear industry.

Partly as a response to this, ASEA and the Swedish Federation of Industries presented an energy program of their own, calling for a total of roughly twenty reactors by the mid-1990s, together with measures to stimulate electric space-heating and such changes in the electricity taxation system that would stimulate demand for electricity. This program has been backed by the Swedish electric power industry.

Solar Sweden

The proposals of ASEA and others can be seen as the continuation of a path that represents conventional wisdom in Sweden since the late 1950s. In terms of the Energy Commission, it very much resembles the D alternative.

However, the Energy Commission did not analyze the long-term implications of the four alternatives nor where present conditions lead.

These issues are addressed in another study, made by the Secretariat for Future Studies. Two different indigenous supply alternatives have been studied, one based entirely on nuclear and one entirely on solar energy. The object was to determine what characteristics a medium-term policy oriented toward long-term freedom of action had to have. Thus it was sufficient to study the extreme alternatives. Any midterm policy that is adaptable to extremes should be automatically adaptable to combinations. In this chapter we present only the solar case.

The major reason for the Solar-Sweden study is that the concept is a popular one; in the Swedish energy debate there has been much wishful thinking about the promises of renewable energy systems. Proponents of existing energy systems, however, have ridiculed the idea—equally without substantial evidence. But no one actually has made an attempt to see what a solar system might look like.

Some aspects favoring a Solar Sweden are high technological competence, large land areas available for biomass production, reasonably high solar insolation (1,000 kWh/m² on a horizontal surface), and a reasonably large potential for wind power. Existing hydropower capacity also facilitates load management.

The following assumptions were made:

— The time perspective is the year 2015, which seems to be a not unreasonable time frame in which to replace imported oil (it took 35 years to achieve the present 70 percent dependence).
— Production of goods and services are assumed to be twice as large as today (which is sufficient, for instance, to give all households the same standard of living as the top 10 percent has today). Population is the same as today (8 million).
— Specific energy consumption is reduced by 20 percent in industry, 50 percent in services, and 30 percent in households (these figures are regarded as conservative).
— Total number of dwellings is increased by 40 percent.
— Hydropower is assumed to be 65 TWh, and the present use of biomass, (wood, bark, and lye) in paper and pulp industry (36 TWh) is also assumed constant.

The data are given in table 14. Overall energy demand is compatible with the forecasts up to 1990 used by the energy commission.

No major technological breakthroughs are assumed, except that fuel cells are used extensively. The system is not optimized with respect to consumption; that is, the energy prices implied may very well lead to stronger reductions in specific energy consumptions than assumed. The mix within the system is not optimized either. These limitations are, however, not serious in view of the type of conclusions sought.

The sources used are given in table 15, together with cost estimates.

The cost figures used reflect 1977 estimates of prototype costs in the 1980s rather than costs of industrial mass production.

The conversion system includes a large number of district heating schemes with or without cogeneration, fuel cells, and meth-

TABLE 14

THE SWEDISH ECONOMY IN THE YEARS 1975 AND 2015

	1975	2015		2015
		Production level	Specific energy use	
		(compared with 1975		
	TWh	percentages)		TWh
Production of goods	165	100	20	264
Services				
Transportation	75	100	50	75
Others	70	100	50	70
Housing including				
household electricity	80	40	30	80
	390			489
Conversion losses	25			79
Total supply	415			568

anol production. The basic idea is to use biomass in as large part as possible as fuel without conversion, or if conversion is needed (as for methanol production) then use the waste heat. Methanol is used for fuel cells for the transportation sector. Details of the supply system are given in figure 14.

The biggest problems in implementation are in land use. Although Sweden is a sparsely populated country, there is no doubt that such a large biomass scheme limits land use for other activities. Wind power may also be restricted by land-use policy. The windy areas happen to coincide with either prime agricultural land or vacation areas. The introduction of photovoltaics and solar heating is more of an institutional problem; large-scale application requires retrofitting existing buildings. Environmentally, the largest unknown is probably biomass, although many seem to view these problems as solvable.

TABLE 15
ENERGY SUPPLY IN SOLAR SWEDEN TOGETHER
WITH SOME COST ESTIMATES

	TWh annually	Units	Cost
Hydro	65		
Wind	30	3700 units of 4 MW each	800 \$/kW[1]
Photovoltaic cells	50	50 m²/capita (400 · 10⁶ m² total)	0,67\$/W[1] peak
Solar heating	71	Community size units	0,4 \$/kWh[1]
Biomass			
energy plantations	260	90 MWh/hectar, 6–7 % of Swedish land area	0,012 \$/kWh[2]
crop residues, marine plantations, straw and reed, waste etc.	55		0,009 \$/kWh[2]
bark and lye	36		
Total supplied	568		
Conversion losses	79		
Total used	488		

[1] Capital cost
[2] Production cost

Nevertheless, a Solar Sweden on the demand level assumed here looks feasible, although it is much too early to claim that it can be turned into reality. Technical concepts in the research and development stage have to mature into industrial production before anything can be said with reasonable certainty.

AN ASSESSMENT

Areas of uncertainty are large. Technological uncertainties arise over several renewable components. The effects on environment

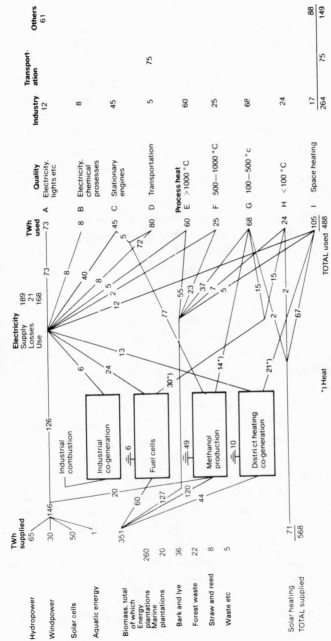

Fig. 14. Supply system.

(biomass) and land use (biomass, wind energy) are potentially great, requiring a certain amount of consensus about land use.

Economically the uncertainties are large as well, but it seems that the energy system is compatible with an increase in the standard of living. This assessment is based on a calculation of the total amount of resources needed to implement the system.

The total amount of manpower needed is roughly three times the amount used today, reflecting the high cost of solar energy relative to oil. This increase in the cost of energy is not incompatible with a higher standard of living, however.

Provided the productivity of labor increases by at least 2 percent in general and by 5 percent in the goods-producing sector in particular, it can easily be shown that the doubling of the total Swedish economy by the year 2015, assumed as a basis for the study, is consistent with the cost of energy in the solar case.

Technically the solar system differs to a large extent from what is the moment of inertia in the present system. The important difference lies in the distribution system and the choice of secondary energy carriers. The design of this system during the 1980s and 1990s will have important effects on the costs of connecting new supply sources after the turn of the century. This argument can be illustrated by looking at different end uses. The space-heating sector, for instance, is based on a combination of district heating schemes (fueled by biomass, waste heat) and neighborhood heating systems based on solar heating. Electric heating could play a limited role, too. It takes decades to complete large district heating schemes, and thus it is the policy vis-à-vis district heating during the 1980s and the 1990s that determines whether the cost of coupling solar heating and biomass schemes beyond the turn of the century will be feasible or prohibitive compared to such as nuclear electricity.

Industrial energy is based on a variety of sources (see table 16). Thus it is important that industries during the 1980s and the 1990s

TABLE 16
Energy Supply for Industrial Use in 1975 and in Solar Sweden

	Today	Solar Sweden
Electricity	38	71
Oil	71	—
Methanol	—	10
Biomass (direct use)	—	88
Other fuels	51	36
Waste heat, district heat	—	44
Solar heating	—	17
	160	264

invest in flexible end-use systems if the possibility of connecting solar energy at a later stage to the end use system shall exist.

Finally the electricity sector is made up of a variety of sources (TWh annually).

These sources employ rather large technical changes from today's or to what a nuclear system would look like. The electric supply in Solar Sweden is located much closer to the user, is more unpredictable (wind and solar), is more frequently connected to waste-heat use, and thus requires rather different types of load management schemes than does the existing electrical system.

In sum, the differences in technical requirements compared to today's are so large as to suggest that energy policy for the rest of the century must be directed partly toward the development of a distribution system to which many divergent supply alternatives can be coupled. Today's distribution systems do not have these properties, but there does not seem to be any major technical or economic obstacles to their adaptation. The problems that remain are primarily institutional.

TABLE 17

ELECTRICITY SUPPLY TODAY

AND IN SOLAR SWEDEN

	Today	Solar Sweden
Hydro	54	65
Nuclear	15	—
Cogeneration	7.5	19
Fuel Cells	—	24
Wind	—	30
Photovoltaics	—	50
Oil-fired	7.5	—
	84	188

Institutional differences. Large technical differences also imply large institutional differences. Solar Sweden requires integration of end use, distribution, and supply. Land-use planning, both for buildings and for arable land have to be extensive. This means that individual landowners have to relinquish part of their rights —preferably to local authorities. The local authorities also must have the power to coordinate conservation and retrofitting with the expansion of capital-intensive, but inflexible supply systems such as district heating.

Thus it seems that individuals and private enterprise will have to yield some of their sovereignty to public planning if the solar solution, which cannot be implemented without a strengthening of both local and central authorities, is to be implemented. What is true in the case of solar energy is true for nuclear energy as well.

The overall conclusion is that the *institutional infrastructure* of a Solar Sweden differs from today's infrastructure. Thus medium-term energy policy must be directed toward establishing institutions that can carry out these new tasks.

NUCLEAR POWER AND THE WEDDING OF TIME PERSPECTIVES

It is now possible to combine the medium-term perspective of the energy commission and the long-term perspective of the study from the Secretariat for Future Studies. The latter shows conclusively that the uncertainties of the solar and the nuclear long-term alternatives make an open-ended policy the only reasonable one. The former shows that nuclear power should not be rejected in the medium term, although there is no need to go beyond the present program of thirteen reactors. This program, together with some more hydropower, combined generation of electricity, conservation, and (possibly) wind power, is sufficient to satisfy electricity supply till the end of the century. Oil should also be replaced in some areas with other energy sources in this time period, such as natural gas, peat, and coal. The long-term studies also show that a medium-term policy has to be specifically designed to create freedom of action in the long run. Four policy items have to be considered:

Time has to be bought through conservation and the limited use of some other sources (gas, coal, peat) as well as a limited nuclear program.

Flexibility of the distribution system has to be created through careful design of secondary carriers and end-use devices in order to make the different long-term alternatives compatible with the medium-term distribution system.

Solar technologies have to be developed on a moderate industrial scale at least in order to make an assessment of their potential and also to facilitate a comparison with nuclear technology.

Institutional neutrality has to be created, in order to ensure that the solar industries are given a chance to develop.

These four items follow directly from the previous discussion, but the last two merit more detailed consideration.

158 | Nuclear Power in Sweden's Energy Future

Breaking up the Momentum

The challenge that an open-ended energy policy means to a policy maker cannot be overemphasized. Pressures to make decisions and commitments will be very strong from both solar and nuclear constituencies. A flexible policy is a way to reduce uncertainty for governments and the public, but it has exactly the opposite effect on those groups and industries that already are committed: their uncertainty is increased.

Moreover, flexibility and freedom of action must not be mistaken for freedom of inaction. Present circumstances are rarely, if ever, without effect on future developments. There is always a built-in future, a momentum built up by circumstances and sometimes by policies. Many of these may lie outside "energy policy" per se. Thus, if no action is taken, the likelihood is that there will never be more than one alternative.

Problems, however, are not only political but also intellectual. There is no agreement on how different mechanisms for influencing the speed of implementation of a particular technology or for stimulating industrial development actually work. In part this lack of agreement reflects more fundamental disagreements over what the legitimate role of government is in society in general and in the market in particular.

Nevertheless, it is possible to identify a number of mechanisms that work in favor of nuclear energy over alternative developments. One such set of mechanisms concerns a possible over-capacity during the 1980s in the present electric supply sector. This possibility makes the utility sector and the nuclear industry unsympathetic to all measures that tend to reduce demand for electricity, and it also makes investments in other electricity-supply alternatives very uncertain (e.g., combined generation). There is a related and marked tendency among utilities to advocate end-use patterns that are highly inflexible, such as direct electric space-heating. These would ensure the market for nuclear-generated electricity (roughly half the present nuclear program is supposed to be used for electric space-heating purposes).

Another set of mechanisms tends to favor *electrification* over other secondary energy carriers. This is most notable in the space-heating market, which is of critical importance to the demand for electricity and thus for nuclear energy. The medium-term alternative to electric space heating is district heating, both in newly constructed buildings and when the oil-based furnaces in existing buildings are replaced. This district heating could be produced either in large or small plants by different fuels. District heating does not, however, have the same advantageous treatment on the capital market as electricity supply. The expansion of district heating to a new geographical area moreover requires a high heat density, that is, as high a connection rate as possible. If these connections are to be voluntary they depend on the price charged, and this will be low, in turn, only if there is full connection.

A third set of mechanisms favors large-scale utility-operated *electricity production* over small-scale, dispersed production, whether it is done by local authorities in combined generation plants, by industries, or by other means. Partly this is dependent again on the way the capital market works, but it also depends partly on the principles of rate setting and other circumstances. As long as these reflect existing cost structures, they tend to create barriers to dispersed electricity production or, for that matter, conservation. The costs of backup power are related moreover to the design parameters for the electricity-supply system (variations accepted in voltage and frequence), which are tailored to what existing technologies can provide. These characteristics serve partly to guarantee that new equipment can be connected to existing supply systems. The parameters inherently favor new supply technologies that have characteristics similar to existing ones and tend to disfavor others that are less predictable (wind and solar, for instance).

A fourth set of mechanisms are related to the way *local authorities work*. Many long-term solar technologies and those medium-term distribution systems that make solar competitive over the long run require extensive planning by local authorities.

While some are active in the energy field promoting solar and other technologies, others are not. Moreover, because of the financial situation in Sweden investments by local authorities require more external financing than do the same investments when made by the State Power Board. Furthermore the costs of these external financing arrangements are higher. The reasons for these differences are complex and depend on principles for rate setting, depreciation rules, and rules and priorities within the capital market. Obviously these rules, regulations, and conditions can be changed, but the difficulties should not be underestimated. One reason for this is that these rules are themselves part of a larger system of rules.

One of the reasons behind the financing problem of the local authorities is that they generally are rather unregulated and have considerable economic discretion. New and more liberal financing therefore must be coupled with more explicit regulation, which, in itself, would be a controversial step.

The net result is that it may take considerable legislative work to change even simple rules and regulations, because of their interdependence. It is no wonder that technologies that fit well with existing rules or with technologies supported by very powerful entrepreneurs end up being favored.

Industrial Policy and Energy Policy

Nuclear energy has one overriding advantage when compared with solar: a nuclear industry capable of delivering acceptably reliable technologies already exists. Until a solar industry exists with similar capabilities, not very much can be said about the viability of the solar option.

In order to know what a Solar Sweden is about one must travel some distance down the road. Research and development may reduce some of the scientific uncertainties but not the economic ones. This requires production on a moderate scale at least and thus a commitment by industries, investors, talented people, and so forth. This, in turn, will not come about without a reasonably stable market. At the same time the Swedish nuclear industry requires continued expansion of nuclear power in order to survive.

The major problem here is that the competition between solar and nuclear industries tend to destabilize each other's markets. Solar heating systems coupled with electric backup power is one example. The impact of a large-scale solar-heating program would be an increasing kW/kWh ratio; in other words load duration curves will tend to be such that nuclear plants will not be fully used. In a system with existing nuclear plants, electric utilities will have to set rates to protect existing investments, which probably will lead to reduced competitiveness of solar heating over all-electric heating. In a system without nuclear energy, electric rates may be set so that solar systems are stimulated and nuclear systems discouraged.

Wind power, cogeneration, fuel cells, photovoltaics, and many other technologies close to the consumer end may pose serious threats to existing utilities in general and nuclear base-load plants in particular. Differences in lead times reinforce these problems.

Measures to create a solar industry may very well threaten the nuclear industry therefore. Conversely, measures to protect the nuclear industry and the demand for nuclear-generated electricity may very well create an unsurmountable barrier for a nascent solar industry.

Steps that ensure long-term flexibility are likely therefore to threaten short- and medium-term industrial policy and possibly the medium-term financial stability of today's utilities. The reconciliations and balancing of these conflicts is therefore one of the primary aims of a medium-term energy policy.

In the Swedish context such a policy requires strong government commitments both on the national and on the local level. Such commitments are, however, not without precedent, even in the energy field. The introduction of electricity and the electrification of Swedish homes was in many ways a process just as revolutionary as making solar energy a viable option.

Moreover, this type of policy ranges over broad areas. The main thrust is to shift the burden of responsibility for energy

supply from a few national corporations to a structure where local
and national governments are in charge.

Politics of an open-ended policy

Is a policy of flexibility acceptable politically? On the surface
the answer would be yes: there is substantial public support for
basing long-term energy supply on renewable technologies even
if this meant some reduction in the standard of living, according
to one authoritative survey. At the same time, the opposition to
the nuclear program in Sweden has gradually declined, although
it remains strong. Table 18 shows this.

Referendum. One of the pollsters has repeatedly asked the following question "In a referendum would you vote for or against
nuclear energy" with the following results:

	Oct 1976	May 1977	Sept 1977	March 1978	Sept 1978	Jan 1979
For	27	32	35	39	41	41
Against	57	49	46	40	37	43
Don't know	17	19	19	21	22	16

	Early April 1979	Late April 1979	May 1979	Aug 1979	Oct 1979
For	26	35	35	44	41
Against	53	44	46	38	45
Don't know	21	21	19	18	14

More detailed studies show that support depends on the size of
the nuclear program. A survey conducted in the fall of 1977 on
the four alternatives discussed by the energy commission showed
minuscule support for expanding the nuclear program beyond
the present program (eleven to thirteen reactors).

All these studies have shown consistently that women are more negative about the nuclear program than men, younger more negative than older. There are also substantial antinuclear groups in all parties. Moreover, some results indicate that, contrary to the belief, or hope, of many nuclear proponents, increased information does not necessarily lead to more support for nuclear power. One survey done in late 1978 among the engineering community showed that a large majority of engineers favored a completion of the present nuclear program but not going beyond it.

Surveys, however, only scratch the surface. They do not give the flavor of the controversy or its roots. Some speculations may be appropriate nevertheless. Superficially, the controversy has turned on environmental and, to some extent, economic arguments. More profoundly, other issues are concerned: it is not so much a question of whether reactor accidents are more likely than other catastrophies but whether the public places its trust in its own regulatory agencies be they nuclear, chemical, pharmaceutical and so forth. There are, in fact, studies that show that the degree of trust in social institutions is important in determining attitudes toward nuclear energy. That confidence is generally in decline in Western societies.

On this level the nuclear issue is less an isolated issue than a symbol of a wider concern with the lack of democratic control of a number of industrial systems, among them armaments, transportation, chemicals, and (perhaps) pharmaceuticals. The debate over nuclear power contains a debate-within-a-debate, a symptom of the frustration and alienation stemming from present trends in industrial society.

Seen in this light, the nuclear controversy cannot be reduced to a matter of magnitudes of risk. Rather the issue changes from whether nuclear power is an acceptable part of today's society to whether nuclear power is an acceptable part of any acceptable society. It seems possible to answer yes to one of these questions and no to the other—with different combinations in different countries.

Politically, this conclusion suggests that the frustration that may underlie opposition to nuclear power will not easily be satisfied.

The nuclear industry, however, is not without support. On the contrary, it has strong support in important groups in most political parties in Sweden and some sections of the trade unions. Since the nuclear industry is seriously jeopardized by an open-ended energy policy, the strength and determination of the government in its industrial policy is important. As noted, an open-ended policy also requires local and central government intervention with respect to owners of land and buildings, landlords, private industry, the capital market, and so on. Therefore whether a government—even one determined to act—can marshall enough support for these interventions is a vital question. This is by no means certain, since other issues in Swedish politics right now are concerned precisely with issues such as centralization and excessive regulation.

And, paradoxically, this is where the nuclear path has its greatest advantage. Although many agree that it would lead in the end to more centralized interventions in a number of areas than are presently the case, there is no question that the next five to ten years along the nuclear path would require much less intervention than a policy of flexibility would. The reason for this is, of course, inertia.

Thus the issues of energy policy must be seen in the context of more general controversies regarding the role of governments in postindustrial economies.

How technologies of energy supply are perceived to fit into discussions of government/industry relationships, producer/consumer relationships, economic growth and income distribution, control over technological choices, confidence in and legitimacy of established institutions—these issues will shape the transition away from oil. The question of how many cents, pennies, centimes, or pfennig a kWh costs, or even what environmental damage it entails, is a secondary question.

Bibliography

Bergman, Lars and Harry Flam. *Energi och ekonomisk tillväxt.* (Energy and economic growth.) Secretariat for Future Studies. Stockholm, 1976.

Bolin, Bert. *Energy and Climate.* Secretariat for Future Studies. Stockholm, 1975.

Bränsleförsörjningen i atomåldern. (Energy supply in nuclear age. Report from the 1951 Fuels Commission. Parts I-II.) SOU 1956:46, SOU 1956:58. Stockholm, 1956.

Bupp, Irvin C. *Energy Policy Planning in the U.S.—Ideological BTU's.* (In Lindberg, Leon, et al. *The Energy Syndrome: Comparing National Responses to the Energy Crisis.* Lexington, Mass.: Lexington Books, 1977.)

Coal Research I-IV. *Science,* 193, 194 (1976).

Commoner, Barry. *The Closing Circle.* New York: Alfred Knopf, 1971.

Cottrell, Fred. *Energy and Society. The Relation Between Energy, Social Change, and Economic Development.* New York: McGraw-Hill, 1955.

Diczfalusy, Bo. *Energi och inkomstfördelning.* (Energy and distribution of incomes.) Secretariat for Future Studies. Stockholm, 1976.

Dörfer, Ingemar. *System 37 Viggen—arms, technology and the domestication of glory.* Oslo: Universitetsförlaget, 1973.

Eckholm, Erik P. *Losing Ground. Environmental Stress and World Food Prospects.* New York: W. W. Norton, 1976.

Efficient Use of Energy, a Physics Perspective. *American Physical Society* (January 1975).

Emmelin, Lars and Bo Wiman: *Om energi och ekologi.* (On energy and ecology.) Secretariat for Future Studies. Stockholm, 1977.

Energi 1985–2000. (Energy 1985-2000. Report from the 1972 Energy Forecasting Commission.) SOU 1974:64–65. Stockholm, 1974.

Energiprognosutredningen. bilaga 3. (Energy Forecasting Commission, appendix 3.) SOU 1974:65. Stockholm, 1974.

Energy Research and Development Administration, USA. Compiled in *National Geographic Magazine* (March 1976).

Energy resources in Europe. Frost & Sullivan. Abstracted in *OPEC Weekly Bulletin* (May 24, 1976).

Forskning och utveckling inom energiområdet—en global översikt 1976. (Research and development in the energy sector—a global survey. Report Nr 1 from the Delegation for Energy Research.) Ds I 1976:2. Stockholm, 1976.

Fusion Research I–III. *Science,* 192, 193 (1976).

Harman, W. *Notes on the Coming Transformation.* Menlo Park, Calif.: Stanford Research Institute, 1975.

Hubbert, M. King. The Energy Resources of the Earth. *Scientific American,* 224 (1971).

Hushållsbudgetundersökningen 1969. (The household budget survey of 1969.) Statistiska Meddelanden P 1971:9. Stockholm: Statistiska Centralbyrån, 1971.

Johansson, Thomas B. *Om kärnbränslecykeln.* (On the nuclear fuel cycle.) Stockholm: Secretariat for Future Studies, 1976.

Johansson, Thomas B. and Måns Lönnroth: *Energianalys—en introduktion.* (Energy analysis—an introduction.) Stockholm: Secretariat for Future Studies, 1975.

Johansson, Thomas B. and Peter Steen: *Solar Sweden.* Stockholm: Secretariat for Future Studies, 1978.

Kahn, Edward, Mark Davidson, Arjun Makhijani, Philip Caesar, and S. M. Berman: *Investment Planning in the Energy Sector.* LBL-4474. Berkeley, Calif.: Energy and Environmental Division, Lawrence Berkeley Laboratory, 1976.

Kommunal energiplanering. (Report from the 1975 Commission on Municipal Energy Planning.) SOU 1976: 55. Stockholm, 1976.

Långtidsutredningen. (Long-term Economic Forecasting Commission.) SOU 1975:89. Stockholm, 1975.

Ljungdal, K-G. *Bränsle och kraft. Orientering rörande Sveriges energiförsörjning.* (Fuel and power. Orientation to Sweden's energy supply. Published at the instance of the 1951 Fuels Commision.) SOU 1951:32. Stockholm, 1951.

Lönnroth, Måns. *Swedish energy policy—technology in the political process.* Stockholm: Secretariat for Future Studies, 1976. (This report will also appear in a coming book by Leon Lindberg et al: *The energy syndrome, comparing national responses to the energy crisis.* Lexington, Mass.: Lexington Books, 1977.)

Lönnroth, Måns, Thomas Johansson, and Peter Steen: Energy in transition. Stockholm: Secretariat for Future Studies, 1977.

————. Sweden beyond oil-nuclear commitments and solar options. The final report from the project "Energy and Society," to be published by Pergamon Press.

Lovins, Amory B. Energy Strategy: The Road Not Taken? *Foreign Affairs* (October 1976).

———. *Scale, Centralization, and Electrification in Energy Systems.* First draft of a paper prepared for the 1976 Symposium on Future Strategies of Energy Development. Friends of the Earth, Inc. (London 1976).

Makhijani, Arjun and Alan Poole: *Energy and Agriculture in the Third World.* Cambridge, Mass.: Ballinger, 1975.

National Energy Outlook. Federal Energy Administration, FEA-N-75/113. Washington, D.C.: U.S. Government Printing Office, 1976.

Novick, Sheldon. The Electric Power Industry. *Environment,* 17, 8 (1975).

Proposition 1975:30. Energihushållning m.m., bilaga 1. (Government Bill 1975:30 on energy management, etc., appendix 1.) Stockholm, 1975.

Proposition 1976:1 Bilaga industridepartementet. Remissvar på eldistributionsutredningen. (Government Bill 1976:1. Appendix Ministry of Industry. Submission to the Electricity Distribution Commission.) Stockholm, 1976.

Ragnarsson, Per. *Kontinuerliga energikällor.* (Renewable energy sources.) Stockholm: Secretariat for Future Studies, 1977.

Schon, Donald A. *Technology and Change. The New Heraclitus.* New York: Dell Publishing Co., 1967.

———. *Beyond the Stable State.* New York: M.T. Smith, 1971.

Steen, Peter, and Bo Wiman: *Miljövårdens energibehov—ett delproblem i frågan om energi och miljö.* (Energy requirements of environment protection.) Stockholm: Secretariat for Future Studies, 1976.

Thompson, J. D. *Organizations in Action.* New York: McGraw-Hill, 1967.

Tompuri, Gösta. *Energi och u-ländernas utveckling.* (Energy and the development of developing countries.) Stockholm: Secretariat for Future Studies, 1977.

Warman, H. R. The Future of Oil. *Geographical Journal* (September 1972).

Wene, Clas-Otto. *Arbetsmiljö och energi—ett delproblem i frågan om energi och miljö.* (Working environment and energy.) Stockholm: Secretariat for Future Studies, 1976.

White, jr., Lynn. Technology Assessment from the Stance of a Medieval Historian. *Technological Forecasting and Social Change,* 6 (1974).

World Energy Conference 1974. New York, 1974.

Index

Ågesta, 105
Alaska, 17
Anti-nuclear, 163
Appliances, 51, 65, 110, 112
Arab oil-producing countries, 32
ARPEL (South America), 32
ASEA-ATOM, 138, 147, 149
Asbestos, 119
ASCOPE (southeast Asia), 32
Atomic Energy Commission, 105
Auburt, Vilhelm, 122
Automobiles, 33, 65, 68, 75, 78, 83, 85, 96, 97, 98

BBC (Brown-Boveri), 147
Back pressure, 5, 138
Billingen, 28
Biomass, 27–28, 36, 131, 149, 150, 151, 152, 153, 154, 155
Breeder reactors, 25, 35, 36, 37, 38, 85, 95
Breeders. See Breeder reactors

CDL (Swedish Power Producers), 148
Canada, 19
Carbon dioxide, effects of, 76–77
Center Party, 141, 142
Central Dispatching Board, 139
Central Operating Management, 118
China, 34, 82
Coal and coke, 1, 4, 12, 14, 15, 21, 22, 23, 25–26, 33, 34, 35–36, 37, 41, 44, 45, 50, 55, 58, 78, 82, 83, 88, 95, 97, 102, 113, 116, 123, 124, 126, 128, 136, 137, 157
Coal and/or breeder solution, 35–36, 37, 41, 44, 45, 50, 58–59, 97, 113, 116, 124, 126–127
Cogeneration, 148, 156, 158, 161
Combustion Engineering, 147

Commission on Municipal Energy Planning, 133
Communist Party, 141
Companies Act, 119

Developing countries, energy needs of, 81–82
District heating, 5, 39, 88, 94, 104, 105, 107, 113, 115, 136, 137, 138, 150, 154, 155, 156, 159
Dung as fuel, 11, 81

EEC, 85, 98
Economic Commission for Africa, 52
Economic Planning Council (Finance Ministry), 56, 67
Electricity, 4, 5, 11, 12, 13, 28, 35, 37, 45, 46, 48–49, 51, 52, 56, 57, 70, 78, 85, 90, 91, 92, 94, 96, 97, 115–135, 137, 138, 139, 143, 147, 148, 149, 151, 154, 155, 156, 157, 158, 159, 161
  as example of technical and organizational change, 102–113
  sunlight to electricity, 27
Electricity Distribution Commission, 115
Employment Commision, 57
Energy, commercial/non-commercial, 6
Energy Commission, 3, 149
Energy conservation, 6ff, 133, 134, 140, 141, 145, 157, 159
Energy consumption, effect on environment, 73–76
Energy, geothermal, 28
Energy policy, 4ff, 13
Energy, quantity, 11
Energy, quality, 11, 88, 89
Energy Research Delegation, 3

Energy Savings Committee, 3
Energy sources, renewable, 1, 11ff, 13,
    26, 27, 29, 36, 37, 41, 44, 45, 50,
    56, 59, 79, 87ff, 95, 97, 113, 116,
    123–124, 127, 128, 131, 132, 140,
    149, 162
Energy tax, 70, 127
Energy Taxation Committee, 3
Energy usage as it affects real wages,
    68–69
Energy usage reduction, 46–47, 56, 57,
    66–73
Erlander, Tage, 137

Forest, as energy source, 79–80, 81,
    94, 95
Forestry and farming, 60, 81, 132
Fossil fuels, 1, 8, 9, 14, 16, 55, 74, 76,
    77, 83, 105, 128, 138
    emissions from, 75
    See also Coal, Gas, Oil
Framatome (France), 147
Fuel cells, 110, 115, 116, 120, 132,
    150, 151, 156, 161
Fuels Commission, 6
Fuels, synthetic, 26, 29, 33, 95, 126
Fusion, as energy source, 28

Gasoline, 70, 75, 94
Göteborg, 78

Heating, space, 132, 138, 141, 148, 149
Household Budget Survey of 1969, 69
Hydrogen, 90, 92, 93
Hydropower, 1, 14, 21, 22, 27, 28, 36,
    51, 54, 55, 56, 92, 95, 103, 104,
    106, 123, 128, 137, 139, 141, 143,
    148, 150, 152, 153, 156, 157

India, 82
Industry, use of energy, 59–60
Insolation. See Solar energy

Japan, 33, 85

Liberal Party, 143
Libya, 17
Low-temperature heat, 91

Malmö, 78
Methanol, 28, 75, 90, 92, 93, 94, 95,
    150–151, 155

Middle East, 19, 23, 84
Motor vehicles. See Automobiles
Municipal Administration Act, 119

NEPA (National Environmental Pro-
    tection Act), 128
NRC, 143
National Board of Industry, 115, 134
National Board of Occupational Safety
    and Health, 118
National Board of Urban Planning, 52,
    118, 134
National Environment Protection
    Board, 118, 134
National Housing Board, 52, 118, 134
National Price and Cartel Office, 118
National Telecommunications Admin-
    istration, 107
Nigeria, 17
Non-breeder reactors, 25
Norrland, 54
North Africa, 19
North Sea, 17, 19
Nuclear Energy Law, 142
Nuclear power, 3, 5, 6, 14, 20, 21, 22,
    34, 38, 39, 40, 46, 52, 54, 56, 58,
    85, 92, 95, 102, 104, 105, 106,
    107, 113, 114, 115, 119, 123, 124,
    128, 136–164
    as future energy supply, 25, 29

OPEC, 3
Oil and gas, 1, 3, 6, 9, 12, 13, 14, 15,
    16, 17, 18, 19, 20, 21, 22, 23, 24,
    25, 26, 29, 31, 32, 33, 34, 48–49,
    55, 56, 58, 70, 73–74, 78, 79, 80,
    81, 82, 83, 84, 88, 90, 92, 94, 105,
    113, 128, 129, 136–137, 138, 141,
    145, 150, 154, 155, 156, 157, 159,
    164
    natural gas, 19, 20, 24, 33, 157
Oil shale, 19, 29
Organization for African Unity, 32
Otto engines, 94

Peat, 4, 28–29, 157
Photovoltaic cells, 27, 151, 152, 156,
    161
Plants, as fuel source, 27–28
Plutonium, 25, 119, 137
Poland, 34

Process heat, 90, 91
Product Control Act, 120

Reactors, 38, 138, 139, 140, 141, 142, 143, 144, 147, 148, 149

Saudi Arabia, 84
Secretariat for Future Studies, 58, 73, 78, 149, 157
Services, 60–61, 67–69
Siberia, 19
Social Democratic Party, 141, 142
Solar energy, 1, 11, 13, 26–27, 36, 37, 39, 48, 50, 74, 79, 90, 120, 128, 131, 132, 136, 145, 149, 151, 152, 153, 154, 155, 157, 159, 160
Solar-Sweden, 149–164
Soviet Union, 19, 34
Space heating, 38, 67, 138, 141, 148, 149, 154, 158
Stal-Laval, 147
State Power Board, 52, 54, 102, 104, 106, 112, 114–115, 117, 118, 119, 138, 139, 160
Stockholm, 78, 96
Swedish Association of Electricity Supply Undertakings, 97
Swedish Association of Local Authorities, 115
Swedish Federation of Industries, 149
Swedish Nuclear Inspectorate, 118
Switzerland, 129

Tar sands, 19, 26, 29, 35–36
Tariff-rate policy, 38, 111–112, 113, 114, 119, 129, 130, 149, 161
"Technical fix" measures, 47–48
Teknisk Tidskrift, 111
Thermal power, 104–105
Three-Mile Island, 143
Transportation, 60, 67, 71, 78, 79, 82–83, 90, 91, 98–99, 151

UDDCOMB, 138, 147
United Nations, 77
United States, 18, 22, 23, 33, 34, 84, 85, 90, 105, 112, 113, 116, 128–129, 138, 143
Uranium, 9, 14, 20, 25, 28, 29, 33, 34, 74, 83, 84, 85, 114, 136, 137, 141

Västerås, 105
Venezuela, 19, 32
Ventilation, use of energy for, 73–74
Viggen, 51
Volvo Company, 75

Waste heat, 74, 89, 115, 132, 154, 155
Water, 92, 94, 112–113, 153
Water Act, 103
Wood, 4, 6, 11, 12, 21, 22, 78, 81, 82, 87, 94, 136